25 YEARS OF JAZZ

IN THE SPIRIT OF SWING

THE FIRST 25 YEARS OF JAZZ AT LINCOLN CENTER

EDITED BY
WYNTON MARSALIS

PHOTOGRAPHS BY
FRANK STEWART

CHRONICLE BOOKS
SAN FRANCISCO

THIS BOOK HAS BEEN MADE
POSSIBLE BY THE GENEROUS DONATIONS
OF THE FORD FOUNDATION
AND LISA AND DAVID SCHIFF

PUBLISHED EXCLUSIVELY FOR JAZZ AT LINCOLN CENTER
BY CHRONICLE BOOKS LLC.

COPYRIGHT © 2012 BY JAZZ AT LINCOLN CENTER.

ALL RIGHTS RESERVED. NO PART OF THIS BOOK MAY BE REPRODUCED
IN ANY FORM WITHOUT WRITTEN PERMISSION FROM THE PUBLISHER.

ISBN: 978-1-4521-2004-1

MANUFACTURED IN THE UNITED STATES OF AMERICA.

DESIGN BY GARY TOOTH/EMPIRE DESIGN STUDIO

EVERY EFFORT HAS BEEN MADE TO CREDIT ALL PHOTOGRAPHERS
WHOSE WORKS APPEAR IN THIS BOOK.
ALL PHOTOGRAPHS ARE © FRANK STEWART WITH THE EXCEPTION
OF THE FOLLOWING:

© BILL MAY, PGS. 15, 16, 17, 23, 25, 26, 29 TOP, 31

© JACK VARTOOGIAN/FRONTROW PHOTOS, PG. 37

© PETRA RICHTEROVA, PGS. 46, 55, 194

© AYANO HISA, PGS. 60, 62, 73 BOTTOM, 98 SECOND FROM TOP, 104 TOP, 150 TOP, 152, 153, 159, 172, 177 BOTTOM, 185 LEFT, 186, 191 TOP

© BRAD FEINKNOPF, PG. 95 LEFT

© JULIE SKARRATT, PGS. 132 TOP LEFT AND BOTTOM RIGHT, 133 FIRST ROW SECOND AND THIRD AND SECOND ROW RIGHT, 138, 145, 149 BOTTOM, 160 TOP, 177 RIGHT

© CAROLYN APPEL, PG. 146 TOP RIGHT

© PATRICK McMULLAN, PGS. 160 BOTTOM RIGHT AND CENTER, 161 TOP

© JOE SCHILDHORN/PATRICK McMULLAN, PGS. 133 TOP RIGHT, 168

© JOSEPH A. ROSEN, PG. 179 TOP

© THEO WARGO/PATRICK McMULLAN, PG. 132 THIRD ROW THIRD FROM LEFT

THE PHOTOGRAPHERS FOR THE FOLLOWING IMAGES ARE UNKNOWN:
PGS. 80–81, 89, 92, 97 BOTTOM, 154, AND 160 BOTTOM LEFT.

COCA-COLA IS A REGISTERED TRADEMARK OF
THE COCA-COLA COMPANY.

10 9 8 7 6 5 4 3 2 1

CHRONICLE BOOKS LLC
680 SECOND STREET
SAN FRANCISCO, CA 94107

WWW.CHRONICLEBOOKS.COM/CUSTOM

THANKS TO ALL OF OUR STORYTELLERS WHO TOOK THE TIME TO SEND IN THEIR MEMORIES OF AND ABOUT JAZZ AT LINCOLN CENTER.

IN MEMORIAM: TED AMMON, DANNY BARKER, ALVIN BATISTE, AARON BELL, ED BRADLEY, BENNY CARTER, BETTY CARTER, RAY CHARLES, WILLIE COOK, IRENE DIAMOND, HARRY SWEETS EDISON, AHMET ERTEGUN, FRANK FOSTER, CHUCK FRUIT, MILT GRAYSON, JIMMY HAMILTON, SIR ROLAND HANNA, PERCY HEATH, PHOEBE JACOBS, MICHAEL JAMES, JIMMY KNEPPER, JOHN LEWIS, ABBEY LINCOLN, GERRY MULLIGAN, CHICO O'FARRILL, DEWEY REDMAN, CARRIE SMITH, EMERY THOMPSON, NORRIS TURNEY, GEORGE WEISSMAN, AUGUST WILSON, JIMMY WOODE, BRITT WOODMAN.

TO OUR SILENT ANGEL WHO DID SO MUCH OF THE DIFFICULT WORK FROM THE VERY BEGINNING AND ALWAYS OUTSIDE OF THE SPOTLIGHT, DIANE COFFEY.

A PERSONAL AND SPECIAL THANK-YOU TO GENEVIEVE STEWART FOR MAKING EVERYTHING HAPPEN SO SMOOTHLY DOWN THROUGH THESE YEARS AND TREATING US ALL WITH SUCH CARE AND RESPECT AND LOVE.

SOUL 13

THE FOUNDING OF JAZZ AT LINCOLN CENTER

15 **ALINA BLOOMGARDEN**
Cofounder and Former Producer,
Jazz at Lincoln Center

20 **STANLEY CROUCH**
Music and Cultural Critic,
Cofounder, Jazz at Lincoln
Center

22 **GORDON DAVIS**
Founding Chairman,
Jazz at Lincoln Center

24 **ALBERT MURRAY**
Literary and Jazz Critic

FOREWORD 11

11 **GEOFFREY C. WARD**
Historian

KINSHIP 27

INVITING OUR EXTENDED FAMILY

29 **DAVID BERGER**
Arranger, Essentially Ellington

31 **DAVID BERGER**
Arranger, Essentially Ellington

33 **JIMMY HEATH**
Saxophonist, Composer,
and Arranger

34 **IGOR BUTMAN**
Saxophonist, Igor
Butman Quartet

36 **PAQUITO D'RIVERA**
Clarinetist and Saxophonist

39 **YACUB ADDY**
Drum Master, Odadaa!

40 **BILL CHARLAP**
Pianist

COMMUNITY 43

JOINING OUR NEIGHBORS

45 **DAVID SHIFRIN**
Former Artistic Director,
Chamber Music Society of
Lincoln Center

47 **STEPHEN RATHE**
Senior Producer, Radio/
Broadcast, Jazz at Lincoln Center

50 **GORDON DAVIS**
Founding Chairman,
Jazz at Lincoln Center

53 **DAVID SHIFRIN**
Former Artistic Director,
Chamber Music Society of
Lincoln Center

54 **DAVID J. GROSSMAN**
Bassist, New York Philharmonic

55 **TIFFANY ELLIS BUTTS**
Former Ellington Centennial
Coordinator and Marketing Staff

HEALTH 61

BRINGING THE GENERATIONS TO THE TABLE

- 62 **KRYSTAL V. McNAIR**
  Middle School Jazz Academy, 2010–2011

- 63 **MEENA KRISHNAMSETTY**
  Parent of WeBop Student

- 64 **LAURA JOHNSON**
  Former Executive Producer, Jazz at Lincoln Center

- 67 **LAURA JOHNSON**
  Former Executive Producer, Jazz at Lincoln Center

- 68 **ERIKA S. FLORESKA**
  Former Education Director, Jazz at Lincoln Center

- 70 **KABIR SEHGAL**
  Bassist, Former Essentially Ellington Participant

- 71 **PATRICK BARTLEY**
  Saxophonist, Former Essentially Ellington Participant

- 72 **GEOFFREY C. WARD**
  Historian

- 72 **GREG BUNGE**
  Director, Badger High School Band

- 74 **JOSEPH POLISI**
  President, The Juilliard School

- 75 **VICTOR GOINES**
  Saxophonist and Clarinetist, Jazz at Lincoln Center Orchestra, Director of Jazz Studies, Northwestern University

- 76 **AARON DIEHL**
  Pianist, Former Essentially Ellington Participant

- 78 **PHIL SCHAAP**
  Curator, Jazz at Lincoln Center

- 79 **MOLLY WULKOWICZ**
  Parent of WeBop Student

HOSPITALITY 81

BUILDING A HOME FOR JAZZ

- 83 **GORDON DAVIS**
  Founding Chairman, Jazz at Lincoln Center

- 85 **JONATHAN ROSE**
  President, Jonathan Rose Companies

- 89 **STEPHEN RATHE**
  Senior Producer, Radio/Broadcast, Jazz at Lincoln Center

- 90 **DAVID ROBINSON**
  Sound Engineer, Jazz at Lincoln Center

- 93 **LISA SCHIFF**
  Chairman Emeritus, Jazz at Lincoln Center

- 94 **ROLAND CHASSAGNE**
  General Manager, Dizzy's Club Coca-Cola, Jazz at Lincoln Center

- 95 **ROLAND CHASSAGNE**
  General Manager, Dizzy's Club Coca-Cola, Jazz at Lincoln Center

- 97 **GEOFFREY C. WARD**
  Historian

- 99 **IGOR BUTMAN**
  Saxophonist, Igor Butman Quartet

- 99 **BILL CHARLAP**
  Pianist

- 100 **AARON DIEHL**
  Pianist, Former Essentially Ellington Participant

METHODOLOGY 103

THE MUSIC IN ACTION

- 105 **HERLIN RILEY**
  Former Drummer, Jazz at Lincoln Center Orchestra

- 107 **MARCUS PRINTUP**
  Trumpeter, Jazz at Lincoln Center Orchestra

- 108 **TED NASH**
  Woodwind Musician, Jazz at Lincoln Center Orchestra

- 109 **CARLOS HENRIQUEZ**
  Bassist, Jazz at Lincoln Center Orchestra

- 110 **KAY NIEWOOD**
  Director, Jazz Library, Jazz at Lincoln Center

- 114 **BILLY BANKS**
  Production Manager, Jazz at Lincoln Center

- 117 **CHRIS CRENSHAW**
  Trombonist, Jazz at Lincoln Center Orchestra

- 117 **DAVID ROBINSON**
  Sound Engineer, Jazz at Lincoln Center

- 118 **MARCUS PRINTUP**
  Trumpeter, Jazz at Lincoln Center Orchestra

- 119 **RAYMOND MURPHY**
  Tour Manager, Jazz at Lincoln Center

- 121 **DAN NIMMER**
  Pianist, Jazz at Lincoln Center Orchestra

- 122 **TED NASH**
  Woodwind Musician, Jazz at Lincoln Center Orchestra

- 123 **ALI JACKSON**
  Drummer, Jazz at Lincoln Center Orchestra

- 125 **SUSAN JOHN**
  Former Director of Touring, Jazz at Lincoln Center

- 126 **JOE TEMPERLEY**
  Saxophonist, Jazz at Lincoln Center Orchestra

WEALTH 129

WORKING AS ONE

131 ROBERT APPEL
Chairman, Jazz at Lincoln Center

PURPOSE 139

SERVING THE PEOPLE, THE MUSIC, AND THE MUSICIANS

141 GEOFF WARD
Historian

142 TODD BARKAN
Artistic Director, Dizzy's Club Coca-Cola, Jazz at Lincoln Center

143 DIANNE REEVES
Vocalist

144 ANDRÉ KIMO STONE GUESS
Former Vice President and Producer, Jazz at Lincoln Center

152 ROSEMARY RUTLEDGE
Director of Visitors Services, Jazz at Lincoln Center

COMMUNICATIONS 155

RAISING VOICES IN SUPPORT OF JAZZ

159 ASHLEY SCHIFF
Chair of Fundraising Gala Committee, Jazz at Lincoln Center

INTEGRITY 163

BELIEVING IN THE HIGHEST OF STANDARDS

164 MARCUS ROBERTS
Pianist, Assistant Professor of Jazz Studies, Florida State University

166 CHRISTA TETER
Former Production Manager, Jazz at Lincoln Center

168 HUGHLYN FIERCE
Former President and CEO, Jazz at Lincoln Center

IDENTITY 173

DOCUMENTING OUR DEEDS

175 MARY FIANCE
Director of Public Relations, Jazz at Lincoln Center

LEGACY 187

SWINGING INTO THE NEXT TWENTY-FIVE YEARS

189 MICHAEL MWENSO
Vocalist, Curator/Programming Associate, Jazz at Lincoln Center

190 JONO GASPARRO
Manager, Research and New Initiatives–Education, Jazz at Lincoln Center

192 MARCUS PRINTUP
Trumpeter, Jazz at Lincoln Center Orchestra

193 DAVID BERGER
Arranger, Essentially Ellington

194 ERICA VON KLEIST
Saxophonist, Former Essentially Ellington Participant

CODA 197

FORWARD THE MOMENTUM

197 GREG SCHOLL
Executive Director, Jazz at Lincoln Center

198 INDEX

FOREWORD

THIS IS A BOOK OF MEMORIES ABOUT AN EXTRAORDINARY TIME IN JAZZ HISTORY, a time no one twenty-five years ago could have predicted. Jazz at Lincoln Center is the product of one man's clear vision and still clearer focus, but as this collection makes evident it is the handiwork of a host of people of all ages and colors and genders and enthusiasms whose lives have been transformed by it, even as they have helped transform the lives of others.

There has been a lot of talk about whether there is—or should be—a jazz canon. *Merriam-Webster's* dictionary gives its seventh definition of canon as "a contrapuntal musical composition in which each successively entering voice presents the initial theme transformed in a strictly consistent way."

For me, that's the kind of canon Jazz at Lincoln Center embodies: The compositions are great, but the transformations are what matters, and the strict consistency is to be found in excellence and swing.

GEOFFREY C. WARD
HISTORIAN

OPPOSITE: Walter Blanding demonstrates John Coltrane "walking the bar" at a Jazz for Young People performance in 2002.

WYNTON MARSALIS, COFOUNDER AND ARTISTIC DIRECTOR, JAZZ AT LINCOLN CENTER

AND THEN, LATE IN THE TWENTIETH CENTURY, SOME PEOPLE decided to do something about the meaning and purpose of their national music. In the most progressive city in the world, an almost imperceptible shift in attitude was soon to become a movement. It was the latest innovation in the music of freedom: jazz music. Ironically, most of these innovators didn't even own instruments. Jazz at Lincoln Center began as three concerts initiated by a lady from Long Beach, New York, with a social vision.

ALINA BLOOMGARDEN
COFOUNDER AND
FORMER PRODUCER
JAZZ AT LINCOLN CENTER

A FEELING EXPERIENCE BROUGHT ME TO JAZZ.

The winter before I started my years at Lincoln Center, I would meet a friend at Barry Harris's Jazz Cultural Theatre after long hours of work as a senior exec at Macy's. At Twenty-Fifth Street and Eighth Avenue, Barry's was a homecoming and a healing. Blacks and whites mingled with uncommon ease, the food was homemade, and the music spoke truth to me. The atmosphere was noble and humble at the same time, and I heard a language more honest than words could ever be.

However, Barry would often break into verbal riffs on the sorry truth that if something wasn't done, jazz would be lost to the next generation and die out. In 1983, two years into my career at Lincoln Center, word was out they were looking for programming ideas for Alice Tully Hall in the summer. That's when I approached Lincoln Center President Nat Leventhal with the idea of Jazz at Lincoln Center, to which he memorably replied, "Write me a proposal."

I submitted three proposals between 1983 and 1987. My first two proposals were rejected; some thought jazz audiences would be rowdy(!). But Nat kept the door open. In February 1987, at the urging of Lincoln Center Chairman George Weissman, he convened a meeting of the usual producers at Lincoln Center—and me. He asked each one for program ideas for Alice Tully Hall in the summer and that's when I put forth the idea of a jazz series.

I thought jazz had a rightful place at Lincoln Center and that America's first and foremost performing arts center could make a difference in how jazz is perceived in its country of origin. I said I thought we could address Wynton Marsalis's vision. Nat asked me to come back with specific program ideas, and only then did I realize he was entrusting me to possibly produce the series.

PREVIOUS SPREAD: Members of the Jazz at Lincoln Center Orchestra in 1992 preparing for a photo shoot with *Vogue* magazine and photographer Arthur Elgort in SoHo.

OPPOSITE: Barry Harris before his solo piano performance at Lincoln Center's Stanley H. Kaplan Penthouse in 1994.

ABOVE: Alina Bloomgarden and Nat Leventhal at a reception at Alice Tully Hall following the Duke Ellington Suites and Blues show in 1989.

SOUL 15

At our first meeting, Wynton agreed to act as artistic advisor and perform free for the first two years. I got him to sign a quickly written agreement, and the first season was approved. Wynton told me to call writer Stanley Crouch, then jazz critic at the *Village Voice*, for ideas and to write the program notes.

Next, I called WBGO and tagged after Dorthaan Kirk until she finally talked to me and generously shared her Rolodex. We always laugh to remember me calling Carmen McRae, who could be rough, and in my naïveté saying, "Hello, Carmen? This is Alina. We're doing a tribute to Monk at Lincoln Center and would like to feature you." When she barked her assent, we were off to the first season of Classical Jazz at Lincoln Center.

It's great to recall some highlights of those first seasons. Who still remembers: Red Rodney, the trumpeter with Charlie Parker, standing center stage at Alice Tully Hall saying, "This is the best jazz festival in the world"; Dizzy and Benny Carter together at Benny's eightieth birthday concert; Michael White and Wynton and Marcus Roberts bringing Jelly Roll Morton and King Oliver into that hallowed hall; the great pianists—Hank Jones, Walter Davis Jr., Tommy Flanagan, and Barry Harris, to name a few; Johnny Griffin, Sweets Edison, Max Roach, Roy Haynes, all the Heath brothers, Sphere and Abbey Lincoln; Betty Carter, Marian McPartland, Shirley Horn, Anita O'Day, and Jon Hendricks and the convening of the first Classical Jazz Orchestra with Ellington band alumni from all over the world?

We opened in August 1987 with a three-concert series and commissioned artwork from the inspired pencil artist Harry Pincus, whose portraits of jazz greats adorned our posters, and, along with Stanley's writings, became a signature element of those first seasons, giving context and depth to the programs. We sold out every concert and reveled in glowing reviews; *The New York Times* called Classical Jazz "The most important jazz festival in America." WBGO was our partner, and its DJs our MCs, but I always began the concerts with a welcome and can still feel the energy coming out of the dark from those powerfully appreciative audiences.

ABOVE, TOP: Betty Carter in front of an advertisement for the Alice Tully Hall with Classical Jazz series in 1987.

ABOVE: Dorthaan Kirk, special events and community relations coordinator of WBGO, and Alina Bloomgarden, JALC cofounder, backstage at Alice Tully Hall in 1987.

RIGHT: Harry "Sweets" Edison taking a break from rehearsing for the 1988 Standards on Horn performance at Alice Tully Hall.

BELOW: Benny Carter, alto saxophonist, Dizzy Gillespie, trumpeter, and Ray Brown, bassist, performing at the Happy Birthday Benny Carter show at Alice Tully Hall in 1989.

CLASSICAL JAZZ AT LINCOLN CENTER 1987–1990

1987

ALL EVENTS AT ALICE TULLY HALL, 8 P.M.

8/3 LADIES FIRST
Betty Carter, Sasha Daltonn, Marian McPartland, Carrie Smith with the Bross Townsend Trio, and Janis Siegel of the Manhattan Transfer

8/4 THE MUSIC OF THELONIOUS MONK
Walter Davis Jr., Barry Harris, Carmen McRae, Marcus Roberts, and Sphere (Kenny Barron, Ben Riley, Charlie Rouse, Buster Williams)

8/5 "BIRD NIGHT" TRIBUTE TO CHARLIE PARKER
Tommy Flanagan, Roy Haynes, Percy Heath, Billy Higgins, Hank Jones, Charles McPherson, Jay McShann, Frank Morgan, Vi Redd, Red Rodney

1988

ALL EVENTS AT ALICE TULLY HALL, 8 P.M.

8/5 THE MUSIC OF TADD DAMERON
Dexter Gordon, Tommy Flanagan, George Mraz, Kenny Washington and Dameronia, Larry Ridley, Benny Powell, Virgil Jones, Clifford Jordan, Walter Davis Jr., Don Sickler, Frank Wess, Cecil Payne

8/6 SATURDAY NIGHT SONGBOOK
Anita O'Day, Jon Hendricks, Earl Coleman, Frank Morgan, Harry Connick Jr., Joe Lee Wilson, Ray Bryant

8/8 STANDARDS ON HORN
Sweets Edison, J.J. Johnson, Wynton Marsalis, Doc Cheatham, George Coleman, Clifford Jordan, Hank Jones, Buster Williams, Ben Riley

8/9 MAX ROACH: MANY ERAS OF ONE MAN'S MUSIC
Max Roach: His Chorus and Quartet with Very Special Guest—Abbey Lincoln Moseka

8/10 DUKE ELLINGTON TRIBUTE: ALL-STAR BIG BAND INCLUDING MANY ELLINGTON ALUMNI

Trumpeters: Lew Soloff, Willie Cook, Marcus Belgrave, Wynton Marsalis

Saxophonists: Norris Turney, Frank Wess, Joe Henderson, Jimmy Hamilton, Joe Temperley

Trombonists: Buster Cooper, Art Baron, Jimmy Knepper

Pianist: Andy Stein

Violinist: Jaki Byard

Bassist: Milt Hinton

Drummer: Kenny Washington

Conductor: David Berger

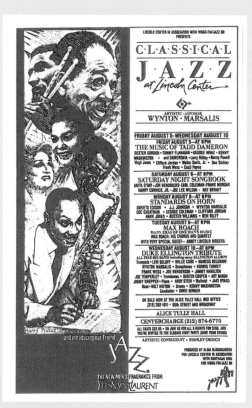

1989

ALL EVENTS AT ALICE TULLY HALL, 8 P.M.

8/4 A BILLIE HOLIDAY REMEMBRANCE: LADIES AND TENORS
Abbey Lincoln, Jimmy Heath, Etta Jones, Houston Person, Shirley Horn, Buck Hill

8/5 BOUNCIN' WITH BUD: THE MUSIC OF BUD POWELL
Original Arrangements by Jimmy Heath, Slide Hampton, and Walter Davis Jr. Also with Art Farmer, Jackie McLean, Barry Harris, Earl Gardner, John Clark, Bob Stewart, Ray Drummond, Kenny Washington, The Tommy Flanagan Trio

8/7 MR. JELLY LORD: THE MUSIC OF JELLY ROLL MORTON
Dr. Michael White, Danny Barker, Teddy Riley, Fred Lonzo, Walter Payton, Herlin Riley, Steve Pistorious, Marcus Roberts, Wynton Marsalis

8/8 HAPPY BIRTHDAY BENNY CARTER
Benny Carter, Dizzy Gillespie, Ernestine Anderson, Hank Jones, Ray Brown, Bobby Durham

8/9 AND 8/10 DUKE ELLINGTON: SUITES AND BLUES WITH THE CLASSICAL JAZZ ORCHESTRA
Lew Soloff, Marcus Belgrave, Wynton Marsalis, Norris Turney, Frank Wess, Joe Henderson, Jimmy Hamilton, Joe Temperley, Britt Woodman, Art Baron, Jimmy Knepper, Sir Roland Hanna, Jimmy Woode, Kenny Washington (Conductor: David Berger)

12/20 AND 12/21 LINCOLN CENTER PRESENTS A CLASSICAL JAZZ CHRISTMAS WITH WYNTON MARSALIS AND HIS SEXTET WITH SPECIAL GUEST JON HENDRICKS
The program will include holiday songs and carols with original arrangements by Wynton Marsalis for his sextet.

Duke Ellington's Big Band Arrangement of Tchaikovsky's "Nutcracker Suite" with the Classical Jazz Orchestra (Conductor: David Berger)

1990

ALL EVENTS AT ALICE TULLY HALL, 8 P.M.

8/3 CRESCENT CITY SUMMIT NEW ORLEANS TRADITIONAL JAZZ
Dr. Michael White, Wynton Marsalis, Teddy Riley, Fred Lonzo, Danny Barker, Gregg Stafford, Steve Pistorius, Reginald Veal, Herlin Riley, Thais Clark

8/4 THE MUSIC OF JACKIE MCLEAN: DEDICATED TO WALTER DAVIS JR.
Jackie McLean, Benny Golson, Donald Byrd, Wallace Roney, Curtis Fuller, Larry Willis, Ray Drummond, Kenny Washington, Arthur Taylor

8/6 BLOWIN' IN FROM CHICAGO
Johnny Griffin, Von Freeman, Michael Weiss, John Young, Dennis Irwin, Ron Carter, Billy Higgins, Kenny Washington

8/7 GOOD VIBES WITH BENNY CARTER
Featuring the World Premier of an Original Composition by Benny Carter for the Classical Jazz Orchestra with Milt Jackson, Bobby Hutcherson, Hank Jones, Ron Carter, Billy Higgins

8/8 AND 8/9 ELLINGTON EXPRESS
With the Classical Jazz Orchestra, Wynton Marsalis, Marcus Belgrave, Willie Cook, Byron Stripling, Buster Cooper, Britt Woodman, Art Baron, Norris Turney, Todd Williams, Wess Anderson, Alvin Batiste, Joe Temperley, Eric Weissberg, Sir Roland Hanna, Jimmy Woode, Kenny Washington (Conductor/Transcriber: David Berger)

EVEN THOUGH STANLEY CROUCH WAS KNOWN FOR HIS sharp-tongued observations, I thought Alina should call him, because he was also known for possessing an even sharper mind. He had deep feelings and respect for this music and was an indefatigable champion of its practitioners. He insisted on the highest quality in everything we did.

STANLEY CROUCH
MUSIC AND CULTURAL CRITIC, COFOUNDER
JAZZ AT LINCOLN CENTER

IN THE EARLY YEARS OF JALC,

the art itself was always the whole point. How much rehearsal time was necessary for a clear and precise performance, how could we get the best sound in the Hall—right there as it was felt and as it was to be experienced from the performer to the audience and back—the perfect course of meaning, execution, communication, and response? All of the planning, meetings, and discussions were focused on the great mystery of all art, which is perhaps a bit more mysterious in jazz because much of it—or much, much more—is improvised than composed. Most art does not trust decisions made in the moment, but jazz does, and fulfills itself at the split-second speeds often detailed in our Internet world, when advertising how well certain machines communicate with each other, making speed an asset rather than a threat or a liability.

But the best jazz playing is also an ongoing lesson about life itself. To improvise as well as jazz musicians do means making empathy so central to performance that a group achieves the deepest aspects of individuality and collective musical form through making audible their sensitivity to one another. Whenever empathy rules the moment, the freedom becomes so great, as Ornette Coleman said, that it becomes impersonal. The great Harold Bloom wrote something about Walt Whitman that could have been said about the blues or about Louis Armstrong, the improvising seer of jazz: "Whitman, when strongest, achieves an art in which celebration and elegy scarcely are distinguishable." All the way from the start to last night, that is what we sought in forming Jazz at Lincoln Center, reaching from the pothole to the penthouse and back whenever necessary. Feeling, refinement, and empathy made sophisticated by a depth that has no special place of origin and no destination other than the human world.

ABOVE: Stanley Crouch, JALC cofounder, and George Weissman, Lincoln Center board chairman, celebrate JALC's installation as a Lincoln Center constituent in 1996.

OPPOSITE: The JLCO in 1992, from left: David Berger, Emery Thompson, Todd Williams, Sir Roland Hanna, Bill Easley, Wynton Marsalis, Norris Turney, Britt Woodman, Jerry Dodgion, Reginald Veal, Herlin Riley, Milt Grayson, Joe Temperley, Marcus Belgrave, and Wycliffe Gordon.

AS IF CALLED INTO ACTION BY THE GHOSTS OF AN ART form whose highest purpose was to raise our country to its own ideals, here came the contribution of Gordon Davis, a former New York City parks commissioner from Chicago who had previously given New Yorkers the gift of community through green spaces, and with him a group of enlightened citizens wanting to affect change.

GORDON DAVIS
FOUNDING CHAIRMAN
JAZZ AT LINCOLN CENTER

SPURRED BY THE SUCCESS OF CLASSICAL JAZZ'S FIRST TWO YEARS of late summer programs, the board of Lincoln Center created a committee in March 1989 chaired by myself, then a member of Lincoln Center's board and executive committee, to consider and recommend to the full board a future course for jazz programming. The other members of that committee were Mario Baeza, William Butcher, Mary Schmidt Campbell, Diane Coffey, Ahmet Ertegun, June Larkin, Wynton Marsalis, Tony Marshall, Albert Murray, Jonathan Rose, and Richard Schwartz. Butcher, Coffey, Larkin, and Marshall were Lincoln Center board members while George Weissman and Nat Leventhal, chairman and president of Lincoln Center, were ex officio committee members. Stanley Crouch was an advisor to the committee.

All of us involved in the early days of Jazz at Lincoln Center waged a self-conscious, systematic, relentless, and occasionally shameless campaign of education, proselytizing, and seduction to ensure that the one uniquely American, up-from-the-bottom art form—jazz—would stand on an equal footing at Lincoln Center with classical European performing arts. And we did that not only because of what we hoped Lincoln Center, with its vast resources and global influence, might do for jazz, but especially because of what jazz would do to Lincoln Center and the broader American cultural iconography. We wanted to infuse American cultural dialogue with some swing and some blues, and make sure that Ellington and Armstrong and Goodman were as much a part of the high art canon as Bernstein, Copeland, and Balanchine.

Many years before these events, when I was maybe nine years old growing up on the south side of Chicago, my father was playing some remastered jazz classics on new 45s he had just bought. Soon, he was listening intently—it was Louis Armstrong's 1928 *West End Blues*. When it ended he turned to me and said with a matter-of-fact certitude, "That may be the greatest thing American civilization has ever created." Indeed.

OPPOSITE: Gordon Davis preparing to deliver a speech at JALC in 2000.

ABOVE: The Duke Ellington Tribute at Alice Tully Hall in 1988, from left: Todd Williams, tenor saxophonist, Art Baron, trombonist, Britt Woodman, trombonist, Marcus Belgrave, trumpeter, Jimmy Hamilton, clarinetist, Wynton Marsalis, Jimmy Knepper, trombonist, Norris Turney, alto saxophonist, Frank Wess, tenor saxophonist.

RIGHT: Ron Carter, bassist, and Gerry Mulligan, baritone saxophonist, discussing the arrangement for "Whisper Not" in 1994.

I HAD NO IDEA OF WHAT JALC WOULD BECOME. AT THAT TIME, we produced three summer concerts a year. I was playing almost 200 gigs a year. It was not a big commitment.

There were those who believed that an institution would be anti-jazz, anti-freedom, and, perhaps ignorantly, I was one of them. But up in Harlem there was a man from Alabama who wrote the book on the blues. He sat under a mountain of books and possessed a wisdom and mastery of subjects as diverse as military strategy, Eastern mythology, and Southern moonshine. He laid the foundation for our institutional aspirations. It was written down "as told to" by a New Orleans boy sitting in the front parlor with his Mobile grandfather, Albert Murray.

ALBERT MURRAY
LITERARY AND JAZZ CRITIC

THE INSTITUTION SHOULD HAVE FOUR BASIC COMPONENTS.

Curatorial: Present concerts, lectures, films, and events. Educational: Teach people of all ages to know how to appreciate what you curate. Ceremonial: Hold regular celebrations, give awards, and maintain definitive traditions. Archival: Cultivate and maintain a library and memorialize what has been achieved.

TO THIS FOUNDATION WE ADDED:
1. no segregation; 2. no generation gap; 3. all jazz is modern. That's what we live by.

LEFT: Historian Albert Murray in 1992.

OPPOSITE: Abbey Lincoln performing at A Billie Holiday Remembrance show with Jimmy Heath in 1989.

PREVIOUS SPREAD: Trombonists Wycliffe Gordon, Al Grey, and Slide Hampton in 1994.

AT EIGHTEEN, I FILLED IN FOR TRUMPETER DAVE BERGER IN an orchestra performing for Alvin Ailey American Dance Theater. I had never played with a plunger mute, didn't know the Ellington style, and had no idea there was a Berger. When Dave returned to the orchestra he asked, "How was the kid?" "Not as good as you," was the answer. Here he was, nine years later, seated before me, talking about that same Duke Ellington whose music I had butchered.

DAVID BERGER
ARRANGER
ESSENTIALLY ELLINGTON

ABOVE, TOP: David Berger and Wynton Marsalis in 1989.

ABOVE, BOTTOM: Rob Gibson, former director, Gordon Davis, founding chairman, and Wynton Marsalis pose in front of the Lincoln Center campus in 1999.

OPPOSITE, TOP: Wynton Marsalis, pianist Renee Rosnes, and saxophonists Wess Anderson, Sherman Irby, and Bill Easley at a 1997 rehearsal.

OPPOSITE, BOTTOM: Ronald Westley, trombonist, Eric Reed, pianist, John Lewis, pianist, and Victor Goines, saxophonist.

IN THE FALL OF 1988,

at the first meeting to discuss performing a concert of Duke Ellington's music as part of the upcoming summer series, Classical Jazz, I told Wynton, Stanley, and Alina that I would transcribe Ellington's scores from his recordings and have the performers find themselves in the music (in the same manner that Ellington's musicians did). I did not want to re-create anything. Wynton agreed. When he asked about personnel, I mentioned some New York musicians who would understand the music and would be available. Wynton interrupted me, "Who in the whole world would you like?" To his amazement, I started naming original Ellingtonians—Britt Woodman, Norris Turney, Milt Grayson, and so on. "We'll get them." When producer Alina Bloomgarden asked how much rehearsal time we would need, I said we could have one day of rehearsal like every other jazz concert, or we could do it right and rehearse for a week. She replied, "Then we will rehearse for a week." And Jazz at Lincoln Center's ethic was established: excellence in programming, repertoire, and performance while nurturing self-expression in the context of serving the ensemble.

And so we hired our dream band of former Ellingtonians and other greats and sent them the music to practice. Everyone took this very seriously. The fraternal love in the room at that first rehearsal was as powerful as the music. The great success of the performance made it clear that we would produce more Ellington concerts, and gradually introduce more classic compositions and arrangements. Masterworks would form our core and be used to encourage a higher standard of musicianship. Duke Ellington was our inspiration and model.

AND THOSE REHEARSALS WERE ATTENDED BY PEOPLE WHO HAD heard through the grapevine that Duke's music was being played. I had never seen that many nonmusicians at a rehearsal. We were on the road to becoming a department of Lincoln Center with a larger annual presence. Gordon Davis charted the course, and Nat Leventhal and George Weissman helped negotiate the obstacles. In order to grow, we needed an executive who understood the music and its possibilities. When we met Rob Gibson, the Southern hurricane, we knew we had a true believer who would make things happen.

Rob Gibson was first brought to my attention when he promoted the septet at a gig in Atlanta. We had played a concert venue, conducted master classes, and performed a free outdoor concert for 60,000 people in just two days. This was highly unusual. He knew how to enlighten and enliven a community with jazz. When he interviewed for the job of our first director, Stanley Crouch and I didn't even need to question him. We knew he possessed the knowledge, ambition, and ability to showcase and produce unique concerts. Rob wanted to present classics and commission new works. Some of the cats called him "country" because of his Southern twang, but he was pure city in his pace, doing everything from growing the staff and programming concerts to packing the equipment truck on tours.

When he came on board in 1991 as director, we were a department of Lincoln Center with a staff of five, including Stanley and me. We went from nine concerts in Alice Tully Hall to twenty-seven events including lectures, children's programs, and film presentations. We played in almost every borough, all styles of jazz from Johnny Dodds to Cachao López to Freddie Hubbard to an original composition of mine called *In This House, on This Morning*.

Still, we were only a department, and we didn't have control over our own budget. Very much like teenagers on the cusp of adulthood. But when Lincoln Center publicly announced its intention to work toward creating a jazz constituent, we had our marching orders.

DAVID BERGER
ARRANGER
ESSENTIALLY ELLINGTON

OUR FIRST THIRTY-CITY TOUR of major concert

halls, the Hollywood Bowl, Monterey Jazz Festival, and *The Tonight Show* in 1992 got more media attention than any jazz tour since the heyday of the big bands. We started every sold-out concert with *Rockin' in Rhythm*. After the final cut-off, I would turn to the wildly applauding audience. I could only see the first few rows, but each person looked as if he or she had never heard music until this moment.

ABOVE: Original members of the JLCO performing at Alice Tully Hall. Back row: Willie Cook, Lew Soloff, Marcus Belgrave, Wynton Marsalis. Center: Art Baron, Britt Woodman, Jimmy Knepper. Front: Norris Turney, Frank Wess, Joe Temperley.

OPPOSITE: Rob Gibson, former director, and Jon Faddis, former JLCO music director, read a *New York Times* review of a JLCO performance.

ABOVE: Bassist Percy Heath performing in 2001.

BELOW, LEFT: Bassists Ray Brown and Reginald Veal in 1989.

BELOW, RIGHT: Singer Jon Hendricks performing *Blood on the Fields* in 1997.

OPPOSITE: Percy Heath, bassist, Tootie Heath, drummer, and Jimmy Heath, tenor saxophonist, performing at Alice Tully Hall in 1994.

THIS NEW JAZZ MOVEMENT REACHED OUT TO ITS immediate family of poets, emissaries, and ambassadors: men and women who made—and lived by—this music. Responses, like that of Jimmy Heath, were immediate and affirming.

Jimmy, who is a master of saxophone, composition, arranging, teaching, and of being soulful, is the definition of a jazzman.

JIMMY HEATH
SAXOPHONIST, COMPOSER, AND ARRANGER

PLAYING WITH BIG BANDS

gave me a thirst for knowledge in terms of harmonies and rhythms that the other musicians were playing. I can't even describe the kind of thrill it was working in Dizzy's big band. Me and Coltrane sitting next to each other and hearing all of that horn Dizzy was playing. This was for three years beginning in 1949. It was a period of fire. It drove you to keep bettering yourself, keep learning, keep digging deeper into the music.

My first commission for the Lincoln Center Jazz Orchestra (LCJO) was in 1994. The performance was on August 4 at Alice Tully Hall. Tenor on Top, an Evening with Jimmy Heath, featuring Joe Henderson, Wynton, the Heath brothers, and my big band. The first half was a presentation of my originals, dedicated to people I love, and standards. It was a heavenly feeling performing with my blood brothers, Percy and Tootie, plus my musical brothers, Joe and Wynton.

The second half was the actual commission, "In Praise from J to J" (Jimmy to Joe).

The concert was one that no one in attendance will ever forget. Joe, who is a great composer, arranger, and saxophonist, was spectacular. The passion and love was running deep, and I thank the LCJO for continuing the music. They know as I do that "What was good is good."

MANY OF THE GREAT MUSICIANS WHO DEDICATED THEIR LIVES TO our art were inspired by the possibilities of Jazz at Lincoln Center. Dizzy Gillespie told me, "Keep that big band going. To lose one's orchestral music should not be considered an achievement." Pianist John Lewis called what we were doing a "miracle." At the end of a difficult all-Ellington concert, he introduced the entire band by name, from memory. He also conducted us in a program of his own music a few months before his death. Even though he needed intravenous fluids during intermission, Mr. Lewis insisted on finishing the show. Heroism of this magnitude inspired us to greater achievements. JALC would eventually invite kindred spirits from all over the world to become part of the movement. In 2003, we brought Igor Butman's big band from Moscow to join us in Alice Tully Hall.

ABOVE: Igor Butman and his big band at their first U.S. performance with the JLCO in 2003.

IGOR BUTMAN
SAXOPHONIST
IGOR BUTMAN QUARTET

IT WAS THERE, DURING THE REHEARSAL, that I was able to appreciate it for what it was, the Lincoln Center community: how musicians, despite the language barrier, experienced little difficulty in establishing a rapport, forging friendships. We suddenly realized we shared "common friends"—the universal idols John Coltrane, Charlie Parker, Miles Davis—people we had never seen in person, but we bonded in our knowledge of them, our reverence for them, an understanding of their philosophy, as expressed in sound.

Those were three phenomenal rehearsals, each lasting six hours. My guys were stunned by the hospitality of our American colleagues and the highly professional manner of conducting rehearsals. This was all in the name of a higher goal: to expand the jazz community, drawing in an ever greater number of people, whether performers or listeners.

The community of Jazz at Lincoln Center has already embraced a great many musicians from around the world. As one of its graduates, I am already stirring things up, creating something here in Russia. This sort of work affords us a chance to forge better mutual understanding, to realize our commitment to excellence.

All this can yield quite unexpected rewards in life.

ABOVE, LEFT: John Lewis, pianist, and Milt Jackson, vibraphonist, rehearsing Lewis's music in 1997.

ABOVE, RIGHT: Lionel Hampton, vibraphonist, and Benny Carter, alto saxophonist, performing in 1996.

YES, UNEXPECTED, BECAUSE JAZZ MUSIC IS THE SOUND of freedom. And when freedom is turned loose, there's no telling where it might go. It showed up in the horn and the pen of a man from Cuba who proclaims a glorious vision of the future with every note: Paquito D'Rivera.

PAQUITO D'RIVERA
CLARINETIST AND SAXOPHONIST

I RECEIVED A SURPRISE CALL AT HOME

in the summer of 2000: "I want you to write a piece for JALC, as part of the series As of Now." It was Wynton Marsalis, who proceeded to explain with enthusiasm all of the details about the series and that the other invited composer would be one of my favorites, the extraordinary trumpeter from New Orleans, Nicholas Payton. I immediately thought of the strong presence of Latinos in the music of the United States, and particularly in jazz. The illustrious names of Juan Tizol, Machito, Chano Pozo, "Chico" O'Farrill, Mario Bauzá, Leny Andrade, Tito Puente, Bebo and Chucho Valdés, Antônio Carlos Jobim, Ernesto Lecuona, Astor Piazzolla, and Michel Camilo came to mind and comforted my ego. Then I decided to ask Cuban poet Annie Colina—in exile for five decades in this country—to write a poem dedicated to the Americas, from North to South, as homage to those artists and their valuable contribution to jazz, the musical genre that I have loved more than anything from my most tender infancy.

Panamericana Suite was the product of that commissioned work, a sort of collage that unites different styles and musical instruments native to this hemisphere, from the Afro-Cuban chants and drums, to the *cuatro* and the harp from the plains of Colombia and Venezuela, the Central American marimba, and the impassioned, nostalgic tango inflexions of the *bandoneón* from Argentina and Uruguay. All of this while a jazz ensemble accompanies a soprano voice singing the beauties of the New World. Premiered at Alice Tully Hall in November of that same year, an instrumental version of *Panamericana Suite* was recorded with great success in the Spanish film *Calle 54* by Fernando Trueba, and the complete version of the piece won a Latin Grammy in 2011 (as best classical composition) on the CD with the same name. *Panamericana Suite* was but one of the many projects inspired and executed at that formidable institution called Jazz at Lincoln Center, whose very valuable staff has finally made obsolete that bitter old joke, "Jazz is too good for America." So let's take that "too" out, please?

ABOVE: Chico O'Farrill conducting the JLCO in 1998. Wess Anderson plays the saxophone in the foreground.

OPPOSITE, TOP: Tito Puente and Celia Cruz performing in 1992.

OPPOSITE, BOTTOM: Brenda Feliciano, soprano, and Paquito D'Rivera, artistic director, during a 2000 performance.

AND THAT KINSHIP EXTENDED FROM THE AMERICAS TO AFRICA, WHERE THE Ghanaian master drummer and griot Yacub Addy first heard jazz as a young child. "Koob," as we call him, was determined to bring the Americas back to Africa through conjuring Congo Square, the eighteenth- and nineteenth-century New Orleans market and playground where slaves and free people of color were allowed to drum and dance. We embarked on a seven-year search for common ground and, upon finding it, wrote a piece together entitled *Congo Square*. Our patron for this, Len Riggio, said, "The work of the Civil Rights Movement is not yet over." This inspired Yacub to tell me, "Yes, brother, Civil Rights is human rights." Because our audiences and our board loved and accepted the collaborations, because our orchestra could achieve the never-before-possible, bringing different cultures together on the bandstand became natural. It was our birthright.

YACUB ADDY
DRUM MASTER
ODADAA!

NINE MONTHS AFTER HURRICANE KATRINA, on Sunday, April 16, 2006, I arrived at the Louis Armstrong International Airport with my wife, Amina, enthusiastic about the week of community residency and *Congo Square* premiere ahead. Immediately, I felt the weight of what happened in the city—I got shivers—and made prayers silently for the many who had died.

The next Sunday afternoon, I arrived for the premier at the site of Congo Square in Louis Armstrong Park. It was the second time I'd been there. I'd visited in 1984, when my group, Odadaa!, first played JazzFest—that's when the vision that would later become the Congo Square Project with my brother Wynton began revealing itself to me.

I walked through the park and so many feelings welled up inside me. I thought about all the slaves and free people who played there on Sunday afternoons so many years ago and passed away; I thought of all those who had passed in the recent storm; and I thought about my own ancestors in Ghana. I went to the statue of Louis Armstrong with a couple of the guys in Odadaa! and we made prayers there. My deceased father was an *okonfo*, a healer, and my maternal grandmother the same. I knew Congo Square had been a center for African religion, as well as music and dance, so I asked the *jinn,* or spirits, to let us do our concert. It was a very hot day, but I was chilly. I asked the guys if they heard something. They said they didn't hear anything, but I heard something like whispers. I went to our trailer dressing room, didn't feel like myself, and was very cold. Then I went back to the statue by myself and prayed again. When I came onstage, the voices became louder, telling me to drum. I started playing and they went away. The crowd was so responsive. The music was still developing, but the spirit of the artists was so strong. It's love that made the music work. If Wynton and I didn't love each other, *Congo Square* would never have worked. We—artists of different cultures—became family. We came together that day with the local community and the spirit of our ancestors to celebrate our common heritage. We created something very special. As Wynton said, "It was powerful."

OPPOSITE: Odadaa! and the JLCO during a 2005 *Congo Square* performance in Aspen, Colorado.

RIGHT: Wynton Marsalis leading his band during a performance of *Blood on the Fields* in Vienna in 1997.

BELOW: Pianist Bill Charlap at a 2002 performance in Dizzy's Club Coca-Cola.

OUR COMMON HERITAGE BELONGS TO all of us and it comes from all music. No one understands this better than pianist Bill Charlap.

MY FATHER, MOOSE CHARLAP,

was a renowned musical theater composer; my mother, Sandy Stewart, is a great singer; my brother Tom, an accomplished bassist; and my wife, Renee Rosnes, a world-class jazz pianist. The musicians I've been around, learned from, and played with are like my extended family. In fact, jazz musicians have a special bond. The seriousness of our purpose is balanced with humor, love, and respect for each other. To me, the goal of music and art is spiritual connection, and the social power of jazz is immense. It transcends our differences and elevates the unique qualities of the individual. Music connects us. I'm lucky to live a life surrounded by music, and it's a privilege and an honor to be a jazz musician.

KINSHIP 41

COMMUNITY

IN WESTERN MUSIC, THE TWO CLOSEST NOTES SPATIALLY ARE THE furthest apart harmonically. When you ride the wave of that kissing dissonance, you're playing the blues. By the 1990s, Jazz at Lincoln Center was a department of Lincoln Center on the path to becoming an independent constituent. We sought to partner with the rest of the Lincoln Center family. Though we shared the same culture, concerns, and campus, we inhabited different social orbits. However, this proved to be a negotiable divide. Our colleagues on the campus embraced us. In this period, JALC brought music to over thirty schools in the five boroughs in collaboration with The Juilliard School and the Lincoln Center Institute; we conducted lectures at the New York Library for the Performing Arts and inaugurated Jazz for Young People based on Leonard Bernstein's legendary programs with the New York Philharmonic. Rob Gibson suggested I write a new collaborative piece every year, so we reached out to the New York City Ballet and the Chamber Music Society. Yes, we were marching toward constituency, but we were not alone.

PREVIOUS SPREAD: The JLCO walks down the aisle of the New York Philharmonic during the *All Rise* premier at Avery Fisher Hall in 1999.

OPPOSITE: Wynton and members of the Chamber Music Society warming up before the *Histoire du Soldat (The Soldier's Tale)* performance in 1998.

BELOW, TOP: The 1998 collaboration with the Chamber Music Society for Stravinsky's *Histoire du Soldat (The Soldier's Tale)*.

BELOW, BOTTOM: Pianist Brad Mehldau performing at Lincoln Center's Stanley H. Kaplan Penthouse in 1998.

DAVID SHIFRIN
FORMER ARTISTIC DIRECTOR
CHAMBER MUSIC SOCIETY OF
LINCOLN CENTER

THE CHAMBER MUSIC SOCIETY OF LINCOLN CENTER

had recently celebrated its twentieth anniversary when I was appointed as its artistic director. Jazz at Lincoln Center was a new concept. We all knew that jazz was going to be a big success. The formula was perfect—America's own great art form residing in the most prestigious performing arts center in the world, led by a visionary genius with limitless energy and stamina. It was breathtaking to watch this launch! Jazz is a natural relative of chamber music, with ensembles that can be any size and its limitless supply of great repertoire.

The Rose Building was brand new! The tenth floor consisted of the Kaplan Penthouse, the administrative offices of Jazz at Lincoln Center, and the Chamber Music Society. It was also home to the Rose rehearsal studio, which served as the primary rehearsal venue for both jazz and chamber music. On any given day we might see Wynton Marsalis pop in to our offices to talk about music, or we might hear amazing jazz coming from the Rose studio. On another day, we might be rehearsing a work of Bach or Mozart or a quartet of Beethoven and see him come by to listen and study the score. The proximity and camaraderie of this setup made it very natural to speak of common ground and ways to work together.

The tangible results of this relationship were extensive and wonderful. The first public events were heard at the close of the 1994–95 season when Jazz at Lincoln Center and the Chamber Music Society presented an extraordinary event including jazz-influenced music of twentieth-century icons Stravinsky, Ravel, Gershwin, and the great music of Jelly Roll Morton and W.C. Handy played by Wynton Marsalis and Marcus Roberts. The centerpiece of this amazing program was the world premiere of Wynton's string quartet, "At the Octoroon Balls," commissioned especially for the occasion. It was a historic event all around. Before the first collaborative concert had ended, we were already talking about the next big thing.

OUR COLLABORATIONS WERE EXCITING AND SUCCESSFUL. We all knew we were bridging a cultural divide, and although we were working with institutions, it was still very personal. The New York Philharmonic was Music Director Kurt Masur, the New York City Ballet was Ballet Master in Chief Peter Martins, and The Juilliard School was President Joseph Polisi. They were more than supportive. I always remember the audience of the NYC Ballet crowding around the pit to hear us play an impromptu tune during the intermission of 1992's *Jazz (Six Syncopated Movements)*. It was magical.

In order to receive an invitation for constituency, an organization had to meet four general standards established by Lincoln Center for the Performing Arts: The constituent must be able to provide a needed service in or to the performing arts. It must set and maintain artistic standards of the highest quality. Its professional leadership must set and hold the respect of experts and the public. And it must have an institutional framework designed to assure financial stability, a commitment to public service, and a dedication to artistic advancement and continuity.

We set out to fulfill all four of them. We built our education program and continued to present all styles, shapes, and generations of the music, tour the orchestra, build the library, and record every performance we could.

By now, there was growing support for jazz throughout Lincoln Center. Our board member, journalist Ed Bradley, hosted a twenty-six-week series entitled *Jazz from Lincoln Center* distributed by National Public Radio to some 160 stations. The producer of those original radio shows, Steve Rathe, is still with us twenty years later and is a part of our identity as much as anyone.

BELOW: Journalist Ed Bradley working on the programming for a *Jazz at Lincoln Center* show on National Public Radio.

OPPOSITE, LEFT: Conductor Kurt Masur listening to Wynton Marsalis backstage at Avery Fisher Hall in 1999.

OPPOSITE, RIGHT: Frank Wess, flutist, performing with the Juilliard Jazz Orchestra at Dizzy's Club Coca-Cola in 2011.

46 JAZZ AT LINCOLN CENTER

I WAS ALONE IN THE OFFICE

STEPHEN RATHE
SENIOR PRODUCER
RADIO/BROADCAST
JAZZ AT LINCOLN CENTER

that had recently housed fifteen coworkers in January of 1991. I was starting to pack for smaller quarters when an important call came in. Although we'd had a critical success with a Peabody Award–winning radio program called *HEAT*, it was off the air due to lack of funds as the recession of 1991 hit the nonprofit world. The phone's ring startled me: "Hello, my name is Rob Gibson," a voice said with a gentle Georgian accent. "I've just come up from Atlanta to produce *Jazz at Lincoln Center*. I know your programs from NPR and your albums—and I'd like to talk with you about making radio from our concerts."

Thirty-six months later, with funding (mostly) in place, and Rob Gibson's assurances to Lincoln Center management that we'd find the rest, we offered the broadcast premiere of a weekly NPR series, *Jazz at Lincoln Center*, with a live performance of Wynton's composition that would become the Pulitzer Prize–winning *Blood on the Fields*.

JALC didn't have its own venue then. It was presenting concerts in Lincoln Center's Alice Tully Hall, and bringing the music to New York's outer boroughs, too. Our radio crew rented gear and we took to the road.

There was Marcus Roberts lifting the roof off Snug Harbor Cultural Center in Staten Island playing James P. Johnson and Jelly Roll Morton; Randy Weston's African Rhythms Orchestra with Melba Liston thrilling crowds in Brooklyn's Prospect Park; Betty Carter (with Ron Carter) bringing generations of the talent she had mentored to Lehman Center in the Bronx; and icons Gerry Mulligan and Red Rodney blowing with the big band on the Tully Hall stage. All of it began to change the perception of jazz in New York, from a few clubs and George Wein's annual festivals to a year-round vital presence in the culture.

At a 1999 JLCO performance in Toronto, we'd just finished the recording and I was winding cables when our associate producer, Paul Chuffo, summoned me urgently to the Green Room. "Just a minute," I said, "there are a few more to wind." "Now," he insisted. "This really needs you." A bit irked, I came, cables in hand, to see what crisis required my attention as we were scurrying to get our gear out of the Hall. I walked in the door to find the whole band assembled around a candle-filled chocolate cake and the legendary John Lewis at the piano counting off "Happy Birthday."

LEFT: Alvin Ailey American Dance Theater in 2008.

RIGHT: *Cotton Club Parade*, the 2011 collaboration between New York City Center Encores! and the JLCO.

IN OUR CONTINUING EFFORTS TO BECOME A constituent, Gordon Davis and the jazz committee were laying the high-level groundwork, Rob and the growing staff were doing roadwork, and the musicians were delivering the message. Irene Diamond, a great philanthropist with the most piercing intellect and unimpeachable integrity, was a staunch, very vocal, and influential supporter. The age-old prejudices against the fine-art aspects of jazz were being laid to rest. Gordon knows the story best from the highest altitude.

EXCERPTS FROM LINCOLN CENTER COMMITTEE FOR THE FUTURE

REPORT TO THE BOARD MAY 1986

"THUS WE CONCLUDE THAT... Lincoln Center should focus on excellence in its core offerings and that no compelling case can be made for adding a new constituent in an area like jazz." Pages 2–11.

RESOLUTION OF THE BOARD OF LINCOLN CENTER INC. DECEMBER 18, 1995

"RESOLVED: That the proposed agreement between Lincoln Center for the Performing Arts Inc. . . . and a new entity . . . Jazz at Lincoln Center Inc. ('JALC'), setting forth the terms and conditions pursuant to which JALC will become a constituent institution of Lincoln Center effective July 1, 1996, ('Constituency Agreement') be, and hereby is, approved as submitted to this Board."

OPPOSITE: Nat Leventhal, Lincoln Center president, signing the paperwork for JALC's constituency in 1996.

GORDON DAVIS
FOUNDING CHAIRMAN
JAZZ AT LINCOLN CENTER

ON A DREARY, MUGGY MIDSUMMER MORNING

in 1995, Wynton Marsalis, Rob Gibson, and I—artistic director, director, and chairman of Jazz at Lincoln Center—met at 8 A.M. for coffee at the now-defunct O'Neill's restaurant on Sixty-Fourth Street across from Lincoln Center. The meeting was to discuss whether JALC, the feisty young department of Lincoln Center Inc., with an equally feisty, very diverse advisory board, was ready to stand on its own and become an independent not-for-profit corporation and Lincoln Center constituent like the Metropolitan Opera and the New York Philharmonic. It wasn't much of a discussion. After only four seasons—four seasons, however, of growing and critically acclaimed programming and success raising money—it was clear to us that we were ready. Next, it would be up to Lincoln Center's board to agree, which it did in mid-December.

How was it that the board of Lincoln Center did a complete about-face between mid-1986 and late 1995 from casting jazz aside as an appropriate or necessary pillar in the Lincoln Center pantheon to embracing it fully as a performing art worthy of Lincoln Center's blessing and canonization as a high-art form? How did that happen?

Constituency was wishful thinking at best when JALC's precursor, Classical Jazz, began in 1987, or even after a jazz department was established in 1990. But we weren't star-gazing dreamers. And it wasn't just our own determination that made the difference. We had something else—we had the music, yes we did—and we had a vision and a transfixing, one-of-a-kind musical pied piper, and out of all that we forged an alliance of old and new, saints and sinners (just a few), visionaries and neophytes, powerful and passionate, and monied and messianic. We never doubted for a minute the joyful, transforming, democratic power of the jazz liturgy, and that assured us that it would finally take its rightful place at Lincoln Center and in the most sacred precincts of art and culture.

ON JULY 1, 1996, WE BECAME THE TWELFTH CONSTITUENT OF LINCOLN Center for the Performing Arts. On the day of our election, Chairman Nat Leventhal said, "We are recognizing today that jazz music has the prestige, the importance, and ultimately the artistry to take its rightful place beside our other Lincoln Center constituents such as the symphony, opera, ballet, and all our other wonderful art forms that are represented here." These were exciting times with a lot to do. In 1987, we performed three concerts and barely had any staff; now, we were scheduled for 150 events a year, in sixty cities, across fifteen countries, with a staff of twelve. Every board member was enthusiastic and very hands-on. Of the nineteen serving at the time we became a Lincoln Center constituent, eleven are still just as committed and proud: Jack Rudin, Lisa Schiff, Hughlyn Fierce, Diane Coffey, Alan Cohn, Michael Fricklas, Ed Lewis, Jonathan Rose, Albert Murray, Gordon Davis, and me. We invested our time and our energy; we nurtured and fought over it, we loved it and we stayed with it.

After achieving constituency, we continued doing the same work—just more of it, and without a safety net. Rob always said it was like moving out of your parents' house. But the Lincoln Center community and audiences embraced us, and the resulting art was innovative and challenging.

DAVID SHIFRIN
FORMER ARTISTIC DIRECTOR
CHAMBER MUSIC SOCIETY OF
LINCOLN CENTER

IT TOOK A BIT OF PERSUASION

to get Wynton to agree to play the trumpet in a complete performance of Stravinsky's *Histoire du Soldat*. The element that made it so much more exciting for all of us was Wynton's interest in writing a companion piece for the same ensemble. Thus the Marsalis/Stravinsky project was conceived. In creating his "Fiddler's Tale," he once again successfully met the extraordinary challenge to write a work that is totally original yet pays homage to its model. Where Stravinsky had worked with Ramuz's fairy tale about a violinist/soldier selling his violin to the devil, Wynton engaged writer Stanley Crouch to write a parallel fable about a fiddler "selling out" to a record producer! Hmm. We toured and performed both pieces narrated by actor André De Shields throughout the United States for a total of fifteen performances. This will always remain one of my most important musical memories and, in my opinion, a very high point in the history of the Chamber Music Society. It was such fun to see musicians like Edgar Meyer and Wynton working together for the first time. It was amazing to see Viennese bassoonist Milan Turkovic playing with Stefon Harris and Wynton Marsalis.

They had to evict us from Chicago's Orchestra Hall because Wynton and Edgar were improvising duets after our concert there until the staff and crew wanted to lock up and go home.

OPPOSITE, TOP: A 1993 rehearsal of *Six Syncopated Movements*, the collaboration between the New York City Ballet and JLCO.

OPPOSITE, BOTTOM: A June 1999 performance of *New Syncopated Movements*, another collaboration between the New York City Ballet and JALC.

ALTHOUGH THESE COLLABORATIONS WERE PERFORMED on big stages, they always created intense personal relationships born out of hard work, discipline, and the pressures to achieve excellence and fulfill the expectations of an informed audience. This influenced younger artists like David Grossman, who in 2000 became the youngest member of the New York Philharmonic at twenty-one.

DAVID J. GROSSMAN
BASSIST
NEW YORK PHILHARMONIC

I CAN STILL REMEMBER THE DAY

when I met Wynton and his septet like it was yesterday (December 10, 1994). I played for him in a jazz master class at the Thurnauer School of Music in Tenafly, New Jersey, as a senior in high school. During the class, he took an interest in me, and that night, to my surprise, he called me up and asked me to play a tune with the septet. I was unable to fall asleep for hours replaying the day's events in my mind (and also because of my freshly blistered fingers). I was blown away not only by the band's musicianship, but by how they welcomed me, a mere kid, into their circle.

He was one of the first people I told when I won a position in the bass section of the New York Philharmonic. In fact, the first week I ever played with the Philharmonic, the Jazz at Lincoln Center Orchestra joined us for a combined program. "An auspicious beginning!" I thought. During subsequent joint concerts of the Philharmonic and Jazz at Lincoln Center, Wynton invited me to the bandstand to play a blues tune with the band as an encore. At one point, when I was going through a trying time in the orchestra, he made a short speech about me during a *Live from Lincoln Center* broadcast. This really raised my spirits and meant the world to me.

LEFT: Rehearsal of "Peer Gynt Suite" with the New York Philharmonic in 2000.

OPPOSITE: Tiffany Ellis at the Ellington Centennial in 1999.

FOR THE 1998–99 SEASON, ROB CONCEIVED OF THE ELLINGTON Centennial. One year of nothing but Ellington. We performed 115 "acts of swing" all over the world, including collaborations with the New York Philharmonic and the New York City Ballet; the production of a book of essays, photos, and newly commissioned portraits of Duke; and a panel with Ellington alumni.

I had a habit of always asking alto saxophonist *extremis fantasticus* Wessell "Warmdaddy" Anderson what we should play before every set. In this, our all-Ellington year, he would say, "It doesn't make a difference. We know it will be great." Tiffany Ellis was the Ellington Centennial coordinator at the time. With a shining personality and a natural ease on the stage, she enlivened and gave context to every event.

TIFFANY ELLIS BUTTS
FORMER ELLINGTON CENTENNIAL COORDINATOR AND MARKETING STAFF

IT WAS ALL ABOUT GETTING THE MUSIC TO THE PEOPLE

and the people to the music. Marketing the arts, and specifically jazz music, has challenges, but when the product is right, the work is easier. Duke Ellington was an expert at audience development and community outreach long before it was called that. In celebrating his birthday, there were endless ideas for events that would lead audiences to Jazz at Lincoln Center. Duke literally provided the roadmap. "Take the A Train" back up to Harlem, to the people and places that had nurtured him and so many other artists.

We celebrated the places Duke and his orchestra played by collaborating with uptown institutions like the Apollo, Schomburg Center, and the Abyssinian Baptist Church. Reaching out to this community allowed us to engage the keepers of the African-American culture that have always supported the jazz tradition. Our mission was to immerse the current community in the experience. So we rode the subway while the JLCO performed with the Subway Jazz Orchestra, and then second-lined up Broadway for Duke's birthday. We hosted a free concert in Central Park with a sweet-potato pie contest won by Ms. Cook. And we summoned the spirit of Mahalia Jackson by featuring the legendary Shirley Caesar performing Duke's "Sacred Music." Find relevant ways to meet the people where they are, and they will come! They did!

I had no idea I'd receive the personal support, love, and mentoring from such masters as Phoebe Jacobs, Albert Murray, the Ellington Orchestra alumni and colleagues of his day, the Ellington family, and so many more. They genuinely and freely shared their time and attention with me, inspired by their love for Duke and the world that his music had created and exemplified. It became my responsibility to expand that circle of friends with the same intensity. Personally and professionally, it was a high point. I learned that relationships are at the core of developing arts audiences.

RIGHT: The 1999 premier of *All Rise* with the New York Philharmonic and Kurt Masur.

IN 1991, AFTER A CONCERT IN Detroit, music director Kurt Masur asked me to write a piece for the New York Philharmonic. Every time I saw him on the campus, he would ask if I was "too afraid." I loved that. His goading challenged me to develop enough technique to at least attempt to write a piece. Though I was doing the writing, all of JALC was involved in the process. The piece required experienced orchestrator/teacher James Oliverio telling me the dos and don'ts and working around the clock on score formatting, and six copyists for the orchestra. At the turn of the new millennium, we collaborated with the New York Philharmonic and the Morgan State Choir. By December my ears were burning hot, I was hearing so much. The night of the premiere, it sounded terrible. I felt as though I had committed a public crime that implicated 120 people onstage, but the maestro stuck with this piece, and later we performed it all over the world. It was called *All Rise* and, regardless of the difficulty, we have been rising for twenty-five years.

A REPRESENTATION OF OUR COLLABORATIONS

The Abyssinian Baptist Church

Alliance for Downtown New York

Alvin Ailey American Dance Theater

The Apollo Theater

Arts4All Distance Learning

August Wilson Center for African American Culture

Ballet Hispanico

Barbican Centre

BET on Jazz

Bloomingdale School of Music

Brigham Young University

Brooklyn Center for the Performing Arts

Celebrate Brooklyn!

The Center for Jazz Studies at Columbia University

Central Park Conservancy

Chamber Music Society of Lincoln Center

Chano Dominguez & The Flamenco Jazz Ensemble

Cinémathèque de la Danse (Paris, France)

City Center Encores!

CUNY Jazz Festival

Festival Productions

Field Band Foundation

Film Society of Lincoln Center

Fordham University

Garth Fagan Dance

Greenwich High School

Harlem Children's Zone

HopeBoykinDance

Hostos Center for the Arts and Culture

International Association for Jazz Education

International Center of Photography

Jazz Aspen Snowmass

The Juilliard School

Ken Burns and Florentine Films

Lehman Center for the Performing Arts Inc.

Library of Congress

Lincoln Center for the Performing Arts, Inc. (Lincoln Center Institute, Lincoln Center Festival, *Live from Lincoln Center*, Midsummer Night Swing)

Los Angeles Philharmonic

The Louis Armstrong Educational Foundation

Louis Armstrong House & Archives

Manhattan School of Music

Mesa Arts Center

Michigan State University

Midori and Friends

Minnesota Orchestra

Murray Street Productions Inc.

Museum of Modern Art

National Endowment for the Arts

The National Jazz Museum in Harlem

National Geographic

National Public Radio

New York City Ballet

New York City Board of Education

New York City Center

New York City Department of Education

New York Film Society

New York Philharmonic

Northern Illinois University

River to River Festival

Savion Glover

SiriusXM Satellite Radio

Skidmore College

Smithsonian Institution

Snug Harbor Cultural Center & Botanical Garden

Southern Illinois University Edwardsville

STREB Extreme Action

Symphony Center Presents

Temple University

University Musical Society

University of Iowa

University of Louisiana at Lafayette

University of North Carolina–Chapel Hill

U.S. Department of State and Cultural Affairs

Washington Performing Arts Society

WBGO 88.3FM

Western Australian Academy of Performing Arts

Whitney Museum of American Art

OPPOSITE: Herlin Riley, drummer, Monty Alexander, pianist, and Hassan Shakur, bassist, perform in the Allen Room in 2008.

RIGHT: Singers Tony Bennett and Jon Hendricks performing at the 1996 JALC gala.

BELOW: Sir Simon Rattle and Wynton Marsalis at the final performance of *Swing Symphony*, a JLCO collaboration with the Berlin Philharmonic, in 2010.

COMMUNITY 59

HEALTH

PREVIOUS PAGE: One of the top three placing bands in the 2006 Essentially Ellington competition preparing to perform at Avery Fisher Hall.

LEFT: Ravi Best, trumpeter, teaching in the Middle School Jazz Academy in 2007.

EDUCATION FOR YOUNG people of all ages is a cornerstone of Jazz at Lincoln Center.

KRYSTAL V. McNAIR, 14
MIDDLE SCHOOL JAZZ ACADEMY, 2010–2011

JAZZ IS LIKE MY OWN SPECIAL LANGUAGE.

It allows me to communicate through my instrument. I wouldn't trade being a jazz musician for anything else, because nothing is greater than music itself. I can find the music in the wind, in the rain, and in anything natural. But the greatest thing about it is that I can give you my whole life in just a few notes.

KIDS OF ALL AGES HAVE INTERACTED WITH SUCH GLORIOUS music and, through stories and examples, absorbed jazz philosophy. They learned how to embrace their own individuality through improvisation as well as how to celebrate the uniqueness of others. Swing showed them how to achieve and maintain a balance with family, friends, and not-friends. Through learning what it means to play the blues, they discovered optimism in spite of the bad times that inevitably find us all.

WeBop is for babies eight months to five years in age, the Middle School Jazz Academy is for sixth to eighth graders, Jazz for Young People and Jazz in the Schools is for second to twelfth, Essentially Ellington for ninth to twelfth, and Jazz 101, 201, 301 are for all ages. At sound checks and after every gig, we work with as many kids as possible. We want everyone with us all the time, from the great-grandma to the little bitty baby.

MEENA KRISHNAMSETTY
PARENT OF WEBOP STUDENT

HANDS DOWN, NO QUESTION ABOUT IT, IT'S CHANGED MY LIFE.

I just wish more people knew how wonderful this class is. We are attending jazz concerts as a family. We've bought albums and DVDs, and are listening to long-lost recordings—for example, Armstrong's "I Get Ideas"—many of which are anthems to the love in our family.

TOP: WeBop kids playing paper trumpets in a 2010 class.

BOTTOM: Attendees from a 2010 Jazz for Young People show at Frederick P. Rose Hall.

AFTER A BEAUTIFULLY executed education event at the Ordway Theatre in Minneapolis, Rob and I discovered the Midwestern dynamo who would become our first education director. In that capacity, Laura Johnson would go on to lead many of our signature education programs with deep feeling and absolute dedication. Later, as executive producer, she organized some amazing collaborations with Alvin Ailey American Dance Theater, City Center Encores!, and the Barbican Centre in London.

LAURA JOHNSON
FORMER EXECUTIVE PRODUCER
JAZZ AT LINCOLN CENTER

IN 1994, I interviewed for the newly created position of director of education, the result of a most generous vote of confidence and commitment from the jazz- and education-loving, take-no-prisoners, this-is-the-time duo of board member Jack Rudin and his wife, Susan. My journey began then as a member of the Jazz at Lincoln Center family, with which sharing the joy of swing with as many people, in as many ways and places as humanly possible, was a way of life.

RIGHT: Wynton Marsalis working with a class of high school students at Orchestra Hall in Chicago.

ON DECEMBER 19, 1992, WE LAUNCHED JAZZ FOR YOUNG PEOPLE: informal, hour-long concerts for parents and kids that used analogies to explain aspects of jazz. Baseline funding came from the Louis Armstrong Educational Foundation led by the dynamic Phoebe Jacobs. For the first season of this initiative, the foundation gave us $150,000 of Pops's money. In 2001, under the supervision of Michele Schroeder and Sandy Feldstein, and with Scholastic Inc., we developed a national Jazz for Young People curriculum with completely retooled scripts and over 100 newly recorded musical examples. That too was funded by Armstrong to the tune of $1.7 million.

We loved to play with and for kids, and the parents enjoyed the participatory exercises as much as their children. Board member Dick Cashin and wife, Lisa, became interested in JALC, taking their now-grown-up kids to Jazz for Young People concerts. "Those are a lot of big kids out there," I would say when parents got too enthusiastic singing a riff. "Wake up, wake up, wake up, sleepyhead. Get up, morning, school time, no more bed." That's how we taught blues lyrics in "What Is the Blues?" For "What Is an Arranger?" the band dressed up cacophonously to demonstrate the impact of a personal clothing arrangement. For a brief period, we invited any kid with a horn onstage to jam. Eventually, there were so many we had to stop. Down through the years, the biggest lesson we learned: Never pass out kazoos to 700 kids at the beginning of a show.

After every show, Laura and I would discuss its merits or shortcomings. Laura was all education all the time.

LAURA JOHNSON
FORMER EXECUTIVE PRODUCER
JAZZ AT LINCOLN CENTER

JAZZ AT LINCOLN CENTER IS A CAUSE, A CALL.

Witness Marcus Roberts teaching a class in a small Wisconsin university, extolling with penetrating force the lessons of swing, then swinging later that night, all night long, changing people's lives forever. Observe Ted Nash, Marcus Printup, Victor Goines, and other JLCO musicians inspiring high school students, only to see them teach the same students in college years later, and eventually all together on professional gigs. Work alongside a staff so dedicated and single-minded that they pull out all the stops to make sure people have a human relationship with jazz, changing everyone's lives forever with joy and commitment.

This Jazz at Lincoln Center family is extraordinary. Challenges, encouragement, even rejection. Understanding when to push and when to pull back are part of the DNA of this organization and of jazz, just like our own families.

OPPOSITE, TOP: Ryan Kisor, Seneca Black, and Marcus Printup with young trumpeters in Yokohama, Kanagawa, Japan in 2002.

OPPOSITE, BOTTOM: Wynton Marsalis is greeted by 500 horns on the Lincoln Center Plaza in 1999 to celebrate Duke Ellington's 100th birthday.

ABOVE, RIGHT: Laura Johnson, former executive producer, at work in 2001.

THE ESSENTIALLY ELLINGTON HIGH SCHOOL JAZZ BAND COMPETITION and Festival is our signature event for young people. Under Laura's direction, it was created in 1995 to enable high school music programs to learn real jazz through playing Duke's music. Each year we provide recordings, teaching guides, expert feedback, and other resources, mostly free of charge. It is JALC at its best, and a life-changing program founded by the generosity of Susan and Jack Rudin. Jack was an infantryman in World War II. Susan is a master education strategist and activist. Citizenship is their middle name, and, in 2012, they endowed the Essentially Ellington program in perpetuity, the first endowment for any of our programs. Every May for the past seventeen years, we have hosted Essentially Ellington. Dave Berger and I have served as judges every year. Our second education director, Erika Floreska, led this program with such infectious enthusiasm we nicknamed it "Essentially Erika."

ERIKA S. FLORESKA
FORMER EDUCATION DIRECTOR
JAZZ AT LINCOLN CENTER

OVER THE YEARS, the JALC education programs have valued community, offering avenues for self-discovery, reflection, expression, and a place to be you every step of the way. Through Essentially Ellington, the strength and joy of community is experienced in all kinds of settings, from a rural school band room to a grand staircase where JALC staff cheer and welcome fifteen finalist high school bands from around the nation to Frederick P. Rose Hall, from a jam session in the Allen room to a warm-up room with mentors offering lasting advice to the festival's concert and awards ceremony at Avery Fisher Hall.

On April 29, 1999, the 100th anniversary of Duke Ellington's birth, we aligned the opening of the Essentially Ellington Festival with a celebration at the Plaza of Lincoln Center. Over 500 students played "C Jam Blues" with the JLCO, making one of the world's largest big bands.

In 2000, the Band Director Academy was launched, inspiring teachers with this music, tools, and passion. In 2006, a documentary crew followed one band's journey through Essentially Ellington and captured its magic for the movie *Chops*, which was screened at film festivals all over the United States. In 2010, Essentially Ellington in the United Kingdom was launched, expanding our community internationally.

In 2011, we held the first live webcast of the competition. As bands played, comments were posted—great-aunts and grandparents, alumni, and friends cheered for their favorites and expressed deep pride. And it extended beyond that sphere—jazz fans from Vienna, Poland, England, and Japan, people in school, at work, at home inspired by the dedication, passion, and excellence of the students they were hearing, called for advocacy for music education, expressing hope for our future. The reverberation from within the walls of the 1,100-seat Rose Hall was now cascading across the globe. More than 30,000 people from all fifty states and across fifty countries experienced the Essentially Ellington community.

ABOVE: Stephen Massey leads the Foxboro High School Orchestra with Matt Muirhead on trumpet.

RIGHT: The sax section steps up led by the clarinet. Students perform at the 2005 Essentially Ellington Festival.

KABIR SEHGAL, AGE TWENTY-NINE, IS AN EMERGING MARKETS financier at JPMorgan Chase, an intelligence officer in the U.S. Navy Reserve, author of three books including *Jazzocracy: Jazz, Democracy, and the Creation of a New American Mythology,* and a bassist. Patrick Bartley, eighteen, is an alto saxophonist who is now a student at the Manhattan School of Music. Both were forever changed by participating in Essentially Ellington.

KABIR SEHGAL
BASSIST, FORMER
ESSENTIALLY ELLINGTON
PARTICIPANT

ESSENTIALLY ELLINGTON IS A TRANSFORMATIONAL EXPERIENCE

because it brings together families and creates a new one. For over three years, I rehearsed regularly with my classmates at the Lovett School in Atlanta. We arrived at school early and stayed late in order to perfect our renditions of "The Peanut Vendor" and "Concerto for Cootie." Through hard work, we became family.

In 2000, when we arrived at New York for the finalist competition, something special happened. Our love of music was shared by other bands, the staff of Jazz at Lincoln Center, and the members of the Lincoln Center Jazz Orchestra. My family had multiplied from a dozen to several hundred. At the competition, there was, above all, a respect for the integrity of the music. It was the first time I'd felt such camaraderie and openness. Everyone wanted to learn from each other. It is school in sound. It is life unscripted.

Today, jazz is my compass with the needle always pointing true. If I take on a new project or adventure, I remember my time during Essentially Ellington. I remember the importance of listening and learning. And I remember myself.

PATRICK BARTLEY
SAXOPHONIST, FORMER ESSENTIALLY ELLINGTON PARTICIPANT

FROM THE MOMENT I ARRIVED AT DILLARD HIGH SCHOOL

in Ft. Lauderdale, Florida, my band director, Christopher Dorsey, instilled a dream. He really wanted us to succeed in the world and become a part of the jazz community, and Mr. Dorsey felt that participating in the Essentially Ellington competition in New York City was the best way to achieve this. It was a huge ambition, and a lot of us thought we would never even travel to New York for anything in our lifetime.

After the competition, when the top three bands played in Avery Fisher Hall, the Jazz at Lincoln Center Orchestra closed out for a final performance. I was not prepared for this. Once the band started playing, even though there was third place, second place, first place, or whatever, no one cared! At that moment, everyone in the audience gathered to cheer the band on and clap together. It was superpowerful and simply amazing. There was not a bad vibe in the room, no matter which band won; people walked away supporting each other and loving each other like family for those four days. After walking out of that room, I knew that I wanted my music to do the same thing. I really understood what community and family meant from that day, and that is something forever branded in me.

ABOVE: Joe Temperley, baritone saxophonist, with Patrick Bartley, alto saxophonist, and other Essentially Ellington students in 2011.

OPPOSITE, LEFT: Solo trumpet performance at the Essentially Ellington competition in 2005.

OPPOSITE, TOP: Atlanta's Lovett School performs at the Essentially Ellington competition in 2000. Kabir Sehgal is on bass.

GEOFF AND DIANE WARD ARE DISTINGUISHED writers and lovers of swing. They have attended the Essentially Ellington festival and competition all seventeen years. They encourage each of the bands as if listening to their own kids.

GEOFFREY C. WARD
HISTORIAN

ROSE HALL CALLS ITSELF THE HOUSE OF SWING FOR GOOD REASON.

Listening to the Jazz at Lincoln Center Orchestra develop, and watching its mostly young players work out their own sounds, has been one of the joys of my life; surely there's never been a band that could play so many styles so well—and with so much swing. But for me, swing's selfless spirit is best embodied year after year at the Essentially Ellington competition, when hundreds of eager young musicians put high school rivalry aside to cheer one another on.

ULTIMATELY, ESSENTIALLY ELLINGTON IS also a celebration of band directors and the sacrifices they and their families make to inspire kids, to develop a community of parents and local enthusiasts, and to give their students more when less is always requested, and even desired. When the band directors come to the stage and the kids cheer them for a long, long time, I am always moved to tears. Greg Bunge is the director of the Badger High School Band from Lake Geneva, Wisconsin.

GREG BUNGE
DIRECTOR, BADGER HIGH SCHOOL BAND

YEARS AGO WHEN I DECIDED TO STUDY MUSIC EDUCATION,

I had no idea that this career or job would be so rewarding in so many different ways. At first, as a young teacher, I simply tried to make a connection with the music, make sure the concerts, parades, pep band performances, and fundraisers seemed organized and well prepared. However, as I matured as an educator, I learned that making connections with the students, parents, local vendors, grocery stores, family, administrators, and churches through our music is one of the most important parts of this journey. Through the Essentially Ellington program, I have learned so much about the process of teaching (jazz), performing (jazz), listening to (jazz), and, ultimately, life. The band program is growing, the interest in jazz bands is increasing, and small groups are sprouting up and performing in coffee shops and for small parties. Church choirs are programming more gospel in addition to the traditional choral music . . . and they are asking the Badger kids to play in their pit orchestras! *All of this* because Badger High School has embraced the music of Duke Ellington and this journey called Essentially Ellington.

RIGHT: A little girl in the audience responds to a Jazz for Young People concert at a 2000 performance in Beijing, China.

BELOW: Backstage, Ernie Gregory asks each band before they go on, "Where y'all at?!" "The House of Swing!" they respond. "What you gon' do?!" he comes back at 'em. "Swing!" they roar. Then they're on.

IN 2001, WE JOINED FORCES WITH President Joe Polisi and The Juilliard School to create a jazz presence at the world's premier music conservatory. Joe, a bassoonist, is deeply engaged with using the power of the arts to redefine citizenship in the modern world. His transformational leadership has recalibrated music education in our country. In planning a jazz curriculum for Juilliard, Joe and I discussed topics as diverse as baseball and sixteenth-century counterpoint.

JOSEPH POLISI
PRESIDENT
THE JUILLIARD SCHOOL

WE SAW JAZZ EDUCATION

in a holistic way, constantly linking one concept to another so that an integrated, truly organic approach to the education of future jazz artists could be developed.

Those conversations with Wynton were some of the most stimulating philosophical discussions I've had during my time at Juilliard. To be able to take the time to dream about what one would hope to achieve was a refreshing experience for both of us, I believe, and I'm happy to report that many of those dreams are now a reality. Juilliard's Jazz Studies attracts young artists from all over the world, allowing them to enroll in undergraduate and graduate degree programs as well as an advanced Artist Diploma program. Our jazz students don't just perform; they compose, arrange, conduct, and develop their own entrepreneurial initiatives. And they are now entering the profession and enriching it through their artistry and idealism.

A MEMBER OF OUR ORCHESTRA, VICTOR GOINES WAS selected director of the Institute for Jazz Studies at Juilliard. Vic and I go all the way back to kindergarten, and he was trained in the down-home method by my father, Ellis Marsalis. He demanded excellence and loved having his students around for every professional occasion. You could see him around the Lincoln Center campus with all five horns he plays in hand and his kids in tow, going somewhere to swing.

VICTOR GOINES
SAXOPHONIST AND CLARINETIST
JAZZ AT LINCOLN CENTER ORCHESTRA
DIRECTOR, JAZZ STUDIES, NORTHWESTERN UNIVERSITY

SEPTEMBER 11, 2001, a day that will forever be associated with the terrorist attack on America, was also the inaugural day of classes for the newly created Jazz Studies program, the result of a collaboration with Jazz at Lincoln Center and The Juilliard School. It provided young musicians the opportunity to pursue a degree of study with the world's most remarkable and accomplished performers and educators, as well as benefit from interactions, mentoring, and performances at JALC. We taught those things that make jazz unique: soulfulness, competition for personal identity, camaraderie, resilience, improvisation, honesty, and compassion. We regularly invited legends such as Ray Brown, Hank Jones, Joe Lovano, Clark Terry, and Benny Golson to provide their views and life experiences to the program. Our success is in the quality of young talent we developed: pianists Aaron Diehl and Jonathan Batiste, trumpeters Dominick Farinacci and Jumaane Smith, saxophonist Jon Irabagon, guitarist Lage Lund, bassists Phil Kuehn and Yasushi Nakamura, drummers Ulysses Owens and Marion Felder, and Jazz at Lincoln Center Orchestra trombonist Chris Crenshaw.

OPPOSITE: Marcus Printup, trumpeter, teaches students during the 2011 Essentially Ellington competition.

BELOW: Victor Goines, saxophonist, interacting with the Jazz for Young People audience during a 2009 performance.

AARON DIEHL LEADS ONE OF THE FINEST TRIOS IN New York City. He received the American Pianists Association's 2011 Cole Porter Fellowship.

AARON DIEHL
PIANIST, FORMER ESSENTIALLY ELLINGTON PARTICIPANT

JAZZ AT LINCOLN CENTER IS TWO YEARS MY JUNIOR.

This is difficult to believe, given that this quarter-century-old arts organization has, at its relatively young age, quickly matured into such an influential cultural institution. It has served as a priceless resource at virtually every level of my musical and professional development. As a member of central Ohio's Columbus Youth Jazz Orchestra, I had a number of opportunities to hear, study, and perform Duke's music via access to JALC's treasure trove of scores and recorded sound. It paid off—we were accepted as finalists in the competition in 2002. Yet, beyond Essentially Ellington's competitive focus, the most cherished prize was the introduction to an extended family that nurtured young artists, an organization that made their vast pool of resources widely accessible. This courtesy was extended during my four years of study in the Jazz Studies program at Juilliard. Jazz at Lincoln Center's doors have always been open to any dedicated musician who is serious about the art form.

My own chronology can serve as a testament to the importance of community. Todd Stoll (JALC director of education), my band director in high school, was responsible for introducing me to New York City in 2002. Wynton Marsalis gave me my first experience touring on the road in 2003, and pianist Adam Birnbaum (Juilliard Jazz graduate) strongly encouraged applying for the Cole Porter Fellowship in 2010.

This is why there is Jazz at Lincoln Center. As Victor Goines repeatedly told us at Juilliard, "Look to your left and look to your right, because these are the people with whom you'll be playing for the rest of your life." So far, he is right. We are indeed one big family.

OPPOSITE: Andre Hayward, trombonist, teaching Essentially Ellington students in 2000.

LEFT: Pianist Aaron Diehl teaching at a Jazz for Young People event at Alice Tully Hall in 2004.

BELOW: Carlos Henriquez, bassist, during the 2008 JLCO residency in Chicago teaching clave in Buntrock Hall.

SINCE 2001, THE SEER OF THE AMERICAN vernacular, Phil Schaap, has taught seventy-five full eight-week courses at JALC under the name Swing University. His encyclopedic knowledge and infallible memory is jazz's answer to the Internet. A pure believer in human verification of information, Schaap is concerned with trying to grow audiences for this music.

PHIL SCHAAP
CURATOR
JAZZ AT LINCOLN CENTER

BELOW: Phil Schaap, JALC curator, teaches Jazz 101 in the Swing University program in 2006.

OPPOSITE: WeBop percussionists at the Irene Diamond Education Center in 2010.

THE ESTABLISHMENT OF LINCOLN CENTER STATED

that the United States had succeeded in fields deemed valid by the Old World. Our American goal, however, was to produce art that blared "This is from the United States!" and have that art accepted throughout the world as high art. It was an Era of Good Feeling. This early period of happiness was primarily due to a wonderfully supportive—but aging—audience, an audience that could recall firsthand the dawn of jazz and its rise to national popularity and then international respect. When Benny Carter played for us at age eighty, and again for Jazz at Lincoln Center at age eighty-eight, those longtime jazz aficionados formed a huge percentage of our audience. Those devotees can no longer attend. The King Is Dead! Long Live The Swing?

An audience may take notice and hope when they hear Chris Crenshaw, thirty, Carlos Henriquez, thirty-three, and Dan Nimmer, thirty, in our Jazz at Lincoln Center Orchestra or follow Essentially Ellington, but where is that audience to come from? What if the jazz musicians of the twenty-first century play the most inventive and swinging solos ever? If no one listens, then no sound is made. During our next quarter century, Jazz at Lincoln Center needs to cultivate a sizable number of new listeners: people who receive the art, not make it; people who understand and love the music; people who are not yet born.

AT A JALC PANEL IN 2003, DR. FRANCES RAUSCHER, PROFESSOR OF cognitive development at University of Wisconsin, said, "There seems to be a relationship between early instruction in music and brain development, and specifically between early instruction in jazz and rhythm and arithmetic." Inspired by those comments, we collaborated with Teacher's College at Columbia University to create a jazz course for early childhood education. It is called WeBop.

MOLLY WULKOWICZ
PARENT OF WEBOP STUDENT

I'VE SEEN THIS PROGRAM DRAW OUT THE SHYEST KIDS,

while providing a warm, receptive atmosphere for the outgoing ones too. The music really takes root in all the kids I know and stays with them.

HEALTH

HOSPITALITY

PREVIOUS PAGE: Jazz at Lincoln Center on Columbus Circle.

ABOVE, LEFT: JALC board members Diane Coffey, Ahmet Ertegun, Shahara Ahmad-Llewellyn, Lisa Schiff, Ted Ammon, David Stern, Nat Leventhal, and Faye Wattleton discussing the new facilities in the Time Warner Center.

ABOVE, RIGHT: Philanthropist Ted Ammon, Wynton Marsalis, and attorney Randy Benn in front of Capitol Hill, Washington, D.C.

RIGHT: Wynton Marsalis in a fundraising meeting with Senator Hillary Clinton on Capitol Hill.

IF BECOMING A CONSTITUENT WAS LIKE LEAVING YOUR PARENTS' house, building our own home was to prove even more liberating, exciting, and traumatic. We knew we were too young and inexperienced, but we had heart and a tradition of success, and we were thirsty.

GORDON DAVIS
FOUNDING CHAIRMAN
JAZZ AT LINCOLN CENTER

THE YEAR 1996 WAS WHEN JAZZ AT LINCOLN CENTER

became the newest, smallest, and most ambitious Lincoln Center constituent institution. It was also the year Lincoln Center Inc.—JALC's parent—proposed building a new, multipurpose performance venue.

By early 1997, many of the other Lincoln Center constituents opposed the new building project, even though it had secured a commitment of $9 million in city funding, and a significant commitment of private funds from an anonymous donor. In the late spring of 1997, I happened to be present for a meeting (as a member of the Lincoln Center board's executive committee and as outside counsel for the new project) with the chairman and top staff of Lincoln Center to decide the fate of this building project. The consensus was that it was time to end the project and the conflict it had spawned. But as those present rose to leave, I said, "Could you all hang around for maybe a half hour?"

"Okay," was the rather skeptical response.

I left Lincoln Center's offices and trotted across Sixty-Fifth Street to JALC's offices. Rob Gibson and Wynton were both there. A little breathlessly, I explained what had just happened across the street and said, "So maybe jazz should do the project. The project has no site but it does have a dowry of $9 million in city funding and a multimillion-dollar pledge from an anonymous donor."

Wynton said, "We must have this hall."

Rob said, "Agreed."

I trotted back across Sixty-Fifth Street and into the elevator of the Rose Building to the chairman's office on the tenth floor.

"So?" they said.

"I went across the street to the JALC offices. We want to do the project."

"You're kidding. JALC is just a baby. You have a tiny endowment," and so forth.

I said, "Can I get Wynton and Rob over here to help explain?"

Ten minutes later Wynton and Rob came into the room. The chairman said, "So JALC wants to take over the new performance hall project we just killed? How could JALC possibly do that?"

Wynton said, "We must have this hall."

Over the next two or three days, whenever anyone at Lincoln Center saw Wynton, he said, "We must have this hall." And by the end of the week everyone who worked at JALC was saying, "We must have this hall." By June 18, 1997, the board of JALC passed a resolution that said, "We must have this hall."

Of course I knew who the anonymous donor was but told no one because I had been sworn to secrecy. And JALC board member Jonathan Rose knew because it was his father, Frederick P. Rose. Jonathan had been involved with JALC almost from the beginning—he had been on the original jazz board committee from 1989 to 1990, had been on the pre-1996 JALC board, and was on the board of the new JALC constituent as of July 1996, when he was also chair of the board's executive committee.

HOSPITALITY 83

JONATHAN ROSE WAS THE PROJECT MANAGER. A RESPECTED developer with a deep commitment to not-for-profit work, he was qualified to lead this *and* it was close to his heart. When New York Mayor Rudy Giuliani, due to a propitious confluence of events, selected Jazz at Lincoln Center as the cultural "constituent" in the redevelopment of the site on Columbus Circle, Gordon prophetically warned Rob and me, "This is a serious and difficult thing to do. It will take many years, and by the time it's over, one or two of us won't be here, or maybe all three." We were in for a ride, but Jonathan knew the road.

JONATHAN ROSE
PRESIDENT
JONATHAN ROSE COMPANIES

THE FIRST TASK WE FACED WAS THE SELECTION OF OUR ARCHITECT. After a contested competition, we selected Rafael Viñoly. And he was just the tiger we needed.

The design of Frederick P. Rose Hall had to meet many goals. Among the many concerns for the three main performing spaces, I wanted JALC to have an extraordinary recording room, a facility designed to match the size and acoustics of Columbia Record's old Thirtieth Street studio that was torn down in the 1980s. That was where Miles Davis and Gil Evans recorded *Sketches of Spain*, where Glenn Gould recorded the late *Goldberg Variations*, and where Bob Dylan recorded *Highway 61*. We wanted it to be acoustically live, warm, clear, and full, but adjustable for a wide range of music. We wanted the space to be inviting, comfortable, but elegant. And we needed to provide the most primal connection between the performers and the audience, so that they became one community. We also wanted to create a generative capacity, where we could record and broadcast around the world. We ended up with four major rooms: the Allen Room, based on the form and feeling of a Greek amphitheater; Dizzy's, an elegant club with reverberant, relaxed warmth; Rose Hall, based on the form and feeling of an Italian opera house with surrounding harlequin light; and a large rehearsal room/recording studio with enough volume to give a glow to the sound of a roaring big band.

To achieve Rose Hall's acoustic goals, the entire hall literally floats on huge neoprene isolators. It is a box in a box. And the Time Warner Center itself was extremely complex, made up of luxurious condos, a fine Mandarin Oriental hotel, Time Warner's offices, CNN's studios, Jazz at Lincoln Center, a collection of restaurants, a retail emporium, a basement supermarket, and a large garage. And every one of us had a tight schedule.

In the midst of this complexity, we had a fire—a workman left a hot plate on—and in the middle of the night, the half-built Rose Hall burst into flames. So our contractor, Turner Construction, had to simultaneously keep everything new moving forward, while ripping out and replacing everything old. And they did it on time and on budget.

OPPOSITE: Time Warner Center construction site in 2001.

ABOVE: Jonathan Rose, right, and Gordon Davis, back, in a JALC board meeting.

LEFT: Wynton Marsalis announces the topping-out ceremony for the Jazz at Lincoln Center construction in 2003.

ROB AND I LIVED THE HALL. ON A LONG plane ride to who knows where, we came up with a set of laws governing the House of Swing.

HOUSE OF SWING RULES:

1. All 100,000 square feet should be syncopated and unpredictable, but not eccentric.

2. No one area is of less value than any other area. Care should be taken with the personality of each space.

3. The entire facility should have a "down-home" feeling, but not a forced informality.

4. Dizzy's Club Coca-Cola will have a down-home groove to it—a place where we can throw parties for visiting musicians, where people want to hang out, have a drink, and listen to some swing.

5. The Allen Room, which faces Columbus Circle, should have the feeling of a jazz parade—you won't know where the band ends and the audience begins. The sound system will be an integral part of this space, and the seating can vary to include terraced seating with interesting angles, bleachers, and movable chairs. The feeling is completely new but also antique—like the sound of Louis Armstrong.

6. Rose Theater: This room will accommodate musical presentations of varying types as well as dance, opera, film, and theater. It will sound warm, golden, and light like Lester Young, Billie Holiday, Paul Desmond, and Miles Davis.

7. The Ertegun Jazz Hall of Fame will be an interactive exhibition integrated into the facility.

8. All of the spaces are designed to accommodate recording.

WE TRAVELED TO DIFFERENT LOCATIONS AROUND THE globe, with the acoustical team discussing everything from proscenium stages to the optimum tail of the echo for jazz. At home, two Steves wrestled with our recording capabilities: legendary Sony Classical producer Steve Epstein and our own Steve Rathe.

STEPHEN RATHE
SENIOR PRODUCER
RADIO/BROADCAST
JAZZ AT LINCOLN CENTER

THE ENGINEERING WAS COMPLICATED.

The mayor was an opera fan and wanted the Hall to be opera-friendly. The whole team struggled to find solutions in the space that would allow the reverberant sound of classical music and the closeness of a jazz club. Remarkably, they managed to do both. And the Sound of Jazz team with Sam Berkow, John Storyk, Russell Johnson, and Damian Doria somehow built three of the best music venues in Manhattan, delivering the "warm, golden tone and tail" that Wynton was fighting for to every seat in the house.

My own area was the recording plan. The architects had neatly incorporated a recording room into each venue, but we wanted something more. Broadcast and the Internet were already an important part of JALC's worldwide presence, and it was apparent to me and Rob Gibson that this future Rose Hall should be electronically "transparent," ultimately as accessible in Beijing as it is on Broadway just five floors below. It looks obvious in retrospect but took months of meetings before we could sell and implement the idea of a central control and origination suite from which we could feed any platform from any of our halls to support recording, live streaming, distance learning, or whatever other options might come along to connect our music with the world.

ABOVE: Construction of Dizzy's Club Coca-Cola in 2004.

OPPOSITE, LEFT: Nesuhi Ertegun Jazz Hall of Fame.

OPPOSITE, TOP: Architect Rafael Viñoly showing the JALC design plans to Rob Gibson and Wynton Marsalis in 1998.

HOSPITALITY 89

RIGHT: Frederick P. Rose Hall under construction in 2004.

RUSSELL JOHNSON, THE DEAN OF ACOUSTICIANS, was most memorable. He videotaped meetings and hardly ever spoke, but was stone-cold serious about finding the perfect acoustic for the sound of jazz. Though not given to emoting, he loved our sound man David Robinson.

"HE WANTS IT TO HAVE WHAT?" "A GOLDEN SOUND." "WHAT THE DEVIL DOES THAT MEAN?"

DAVID ROBINSON
SOUND ENGINEER
JAZZ AT LINCOLN CENTER

It meant a quality of richness and depth. It meant the Hall should convey warmth and intimacy. It should extend the very last beat of the note just so much. Not reverb. Not echo. The golden sound. The responsibility for finding this sound fell to Russell Johnson. And he certainly found it. But it's how he approached it that has endeared him to all of us who worked with him. Russell was a giant in his field and a genius at his craft. But he was accustomed to working in the classical realm. He wasn't familiar with jazz or our orchestra. But he soon got hip. Many a day I'd arrive at load-in at a hall he had designed, walk onstage, and there'd be Russell, flying in (on his own dime) to see what we thought of the sound and feel of that particular space. Cool, quiet Russell. Sitting there, listening. Not just in one place but all around the Hall. Sometimes near me, more often not. But he really liked sitting on the bandstand. Right up on the musicians. And then I began to get it.

He was allowing himself to hear the music from different perspectives. What the musicians heard compared to what the audience heard. He was seeking to reconcile the two. He believed that the proper acoustic environment allowed for the best of both worlds. And this is what he gave us in the form of Rose Hall. Russell was great to be around and learn from. And he would always shoot you straight. I remember one day we were in one of his halls, and as sound check wound down he asked my opinion of the Hall. After a few months of his compliments on my work, my head had swollen 'bout as big as Texas, and I said, "It's really echoey and there's no clarity." Russell looked unsmiling at me and said, "Don't be a putz. I don't design a hall to sound good empty! It's designed to sound good full of people. Always remember that." And though I have since been a putz, I never forgot what he said.

IT WAS ALL COMING TOGETHER. WE HAD THE ARCHITECTURAL AND ACOUSTICAL team we wanted. Jonathan was at the wheel, and the entire institution—board, band, and staff—set out to raise money for the building. What started as a $40 million proposition, with $28 million already raised, was soon to become a $128 million crucible. We hit the ground running and developed the tools to sell the "Center of the Jazz Universe." The pressure was enormous. We were a fledgling institution trying to lift a heavyweight job in the most unforgiving environment. Then we were impacted by several changes and a major tragedy. Rob Gibson resigned in 2000, and Gordon Davis left in 2001 to become president of Lincoln Center. The events of 9/11 struck New York, and then, one month later, our newly elected chairman, Ted Ammon, whom we all loved, was brutally murdered. In that environment of grief, turmoil, and economic uncertainty, we still had millions to raise to finish this building. It looked bleak.

In walked Lisa. No one wanted this chairmanship at this time. Only someone with a fighter's spirit would have considered taking it. She told me, "I hope you're ready to do some work. I mean a pile of it." She wasn't lying. God bless her husband, David, for what JALC put him through. We worked around the clock for almost three years to make it happen, and she was cradling us the whole time. In one meeting, a gentleman asked if he could take off his prosthetic leg. She said, "You can take off whatever you want, as long as you keep your trousers on." When there was a dispute over a large (but small) bronze nude male Botero sculpture planted in the entrance lobby of our space, she told the Time Warner Center developers, "There are racial sensitivities on our board due to the color and inaccurate size of the nude." It was moved. In a late-night blowout, she once told me, "I'm ready to not hear from you for a very long time." The next day, at 7:30 in the morning, "Meet me at such and such in one hour." We once showed up at an 8:30 A.M. meeting with no briefing or office number, each having assumed the other knew what was going on. Yeah, we were out there trying to make it happen.

MY RELATIONSHIP WITH JAZZ AT LINCOLN CENTER AND WYNTON BEGAN

LISA SCHIFF
CHAIRMAN EMERITUS
JAZZ AT LINCOLN CENTER

with a four o'clock appointment to have tea at the Carlyle Hotel. A mutual friend, June Noble Larkin, had known of my love of music, my small recording company, and my wide variety of performing friends. She said, in her own words, "I strongly suspect you will be important in each other's lives," which, in fact, turned out to be exactly the case—and so I accepted her invitation to meet, again, in her words, "this young genius."

Wynton explained, in characteristic Wynton fashion, his dreams of establishing an organization devoted to preserving the music and legacy of jazz, something that had not been done before.

I carefully explained that while I felt his ambitious idea was certainly worthwhile, I was overly committed with family, homes, other boards, and a small recording company where I worked pretty hard on a full-time basis. When Wynton begins his siren song, beware. He has the power, charm, and ability to convince a hungry cat to leave a tuna boat! He assured me it would take absolutely no real time in my busy schedule—so much for assurances. I actually believed him, so I joined the jazz committee—soon to become the board of Jazz at Lincoln Center.

We grew our board into a group of passionate jazz lovers on a mission (beware of people on a mission!). We were successful, we made money, we had fun, we received many accolades and became the young darling of Lincoln Center. We became a constituent of the "mother ship" in record time and all was right with the world . . . for the moment. We then turned our sights to bigger dreams: for a space and performance area dedicated solely to the sound of jazz music. Crazy? You bet! But dreamers have an unusual way of finding a way to make their dreams happen. The beginning of our dreams came true when we were offered spectacular space in the yet-to-be-fully-constructed Time Warner Center. Well, we set to work and found every expert and trade that was needed. But, best of all, we felt we had the necessary financial underpinnings to pay for this adventure. We were running through clover; then, we began the year of 2001—our very own *annus horribilis!*

That year brought cosmic changes in our board leadership, our organization's internal management, and, most important, significant changes in the ever-growing financial needs we faced in order to complete our new home. Added to the horror and devastation of September 11th was the immediate work stoppage of all construction in New York, including deliveries of building materials. Our job was closed down tight and the meter was running! In December of that year, I foolishly agreed to the board's wish that I become chairman of Jazz at Lincoln Center. The challenges we faced were daunting. The building budget grew from approximately $45 million to well over $100 million, and that was only the beginning of the fun. Our building site would experience fire, flood, snow storms (fortunately no pestilence), broken windows, countless delays, malfunctions of every type and kind, and even one death of a construction worker from a flying steel beam. Raising money became the focus of our lives, and our board worked nonstop to somehow meet this challenge. The bottom line is that a miracle of sorts occurred when we opened our doors on October 18, 2004. We were all exhausted with the endless problems, the disagreements, the financial uncertainties, and just sheer work of the last several years. But somehow we had managed to create this first ever, extraordinarily beautiful, acoustically pure performance space for jazz music. Collectively, we felt such deep gratitude to all those wonderful people who had joined with us in lockstep to make Wynton's dream of a permanent home for jazz music become a reality.

The moral of this story is simple: For inner peace and serenity, avoid tea with Wynton!

OPPOSITE: Lisa and David Schiff.

WE WENT THROUGH A SERIES OF EXECUTIVE DIRECTORS struggling to find the right fit for us. This was a very complex job leading a young, somewhat undisciplined organization. We needed the firm hand of an experienced and unflappable executive. Once again, a member of our board provided the type of hands-on sacrifice that accounts for much of JALC's uncommon success. Hughlyn Fierce, a man of integrity, took the reins.

ROLAND CHASSAGNE
GENERAL MANAGER
DIZZY'S CLUB COCA-COLA
JAZZ AT LINCOLN CENTER

ON A MONDAY IN MARCH

at 8:30 A.M., Jonathan Rose came to our offices and informed the building project team that the board treasurer, Hughlyn Fierce, would be taking over as president and CEO, effective immediately. Jonathan explained to us that Hugh used to be senior vice president for Chase Manhattan in Asia, which included eleven nations, 1,500 employees, and $5 billion in assets.

This was music to our ears. We were reaching a crossroads in completing the Hall. The level of intensity needed to guarantee we opened on time required a higher degree of expertise, management, and attention to fiscal detail. Hugh was planning to meet with the project team at 5 P.M. that same day.

Sure enough, 5 P.M. sharp, Hughlyn Fierce entered our offices and introduced himself. He explained how much of a jazz fan he was, frequenting jazz clubs in Brooklyn, downtown, and all over the world.

He wanted the project team, and a representative from each JALC department, to meet three times a week at 8 A.M. in the field office to go over all design and construction items that needed to be completed by June of 2004.

The first meeting was set for the following week. I arrived at Columbus Circle at 7:56 A.M. As I was walking towards the office, I decided to buy a muffin. I came out of the store at 8:01 A.M. and entered my office at 8:02 A.M. I turned on the light and who was sitting in my chair? Hughlyn Fierce, president and CEO of Jazz at Lincoln Center. Great.

I said, "Good morning, Hugh." He responded, "What time is it?" I paused and said, "Umm, 8:04 A.M." He stood up, faced me, and said, "When I schedule an 8 A.M. meeting, it means 8 A.M. It doesn't mean 7:57 A.M. or 6:06 A.M., and it doesn't mean 8:04 A.M. either." As JALC employees arrived at the office, many of whom were upper management, he said the same exact sentence to all of them. I mean *all* of them.

That encounter set the tone for all of us. We knew we were going to open on time under Hugh Fierce.

ABOVE: Frederick P. Rose Hall.

LEFT: Dizzy's Club Coca-Cola.

BELOW: Joe Lovano, saxophonist, performing at Dizzy's Club Coca-Cola in 2008.

IN A MEETING WITH PROSPECTIVE DONOR TOM LEE, HUGH PRESENTED our financial statements. Tom perused them and said they were the best he had seen from a post-9/11 arts organization. Then, he noticed there was no line for Hugh's pay and said, "Why are you not being paid?" Hugh responded, "I believe a couple of years at the end of one's career is very little to give to a music that has defined and focused a large portion of my adulthood." Tom would soon join our board.

Land, air, and sea—our musicians played events in people's homes and all over. The staff laid plans and sold, sold, sold. And as the building went up, guests could take site tours. So many great people like Kareem Abdul-Jabbar, Sidney Poitier, and Yo-Yo Ma came to see our promising new building. Roland holds the undisputed record for tours given, about 3,840. He so deeply believes in the power of jazz that his nightly presence in the Hall is itself an act of integrity.

ROLAND CHASSAGNE
GENERAL MANAGER
DIZZY'S CLUB COCA-COLA
JAZZ AT LINCOLN CENTER

IN 2003, I GAVE A TOUR TO THE GREAT ORNETTE COLEMAN.

I took him through the Hall and gave my "A game," taking extra time to explain the various spaces, the acoustics, the philosophy of JALC, et cetera. Most tours took about forty-five minutes; this one took about an hour and a half. Ornette didn't say a word throughout the whole tour. No questions, nothing. We returned to the office, and thinking I'd screwed up for the entire hour and half, I asked if he had any questions or thoughts. He took off his hard hat and said, "I came on this tour prepared to criticize and judge the whole project, corporate influences and all . . . but I can't. This is amazing, JALC is amazing, and this is what jazz deserves."

THE HALL RECEIVED MAJOR SUPPORT. HERB ALLEN, WHO attended Williams College with Gordon just a few years earlier, supported what we were calling "Manhattan's living room." This became JALC's Allen Room. Irene Diamond championed an Education Center with two classrooms and the studio. Irene loved education and remained a staunch supporter. She was a colorful conversationalist on many subjects. Even in her nineties, she would go to the most avant-garde concerts, listen to recordings, and be prepared to discuss them in detail.

Herb brought Don Keough and Chuck Fruit from Coca-Cola to support Dizzy's Club. Don is the definition of class and Chuck loved jazz and did everything he could to help elevate the music. The Louis Armstrong Foundation supported a classroom in Pops's name. There is a poetic through-line in the use of some of Louis's resources to help build the House of Swing. June Larkin, an original member of the jazz committee assembled by Gordon in 1989, and the angel that brought Lisa Schiff to us, supported the other classroom through the Edward John Noble Foundation. Ahmet Ertegun was also an original committee member. He sponsored a Jazz Hall of Fame in honor of his brother, Nesuhi. Ahmet loved to talk about Nesuhi and their mutual love of jazz and Afro-American music. Tough and forthright, Ahmet wanted a Hall of Fame that would stretch throughout the building. Before a meeting, Ted Ammon asked me how we should approach Ahmet. I said, "Just be straightforward. Ahmet will be cool with this." After we presented the idea to him, he looked straight through us and said, "That's some of the dumbest shit I've ever heard." Ted and I couldn't figure out whether to laugh or be serious, but we settled on serious. After that, whenever we found ourselves in a sticky situation, we would repeat that phrase in homage to Ahmet.

The City of New York, whose $18 million baseline funding made the project real under Rudy Giuliani, had committed over time another $10 million with the advocacy of Mayor Michael Bloomberg. And finally, so many lovers and supporters of jazz around the world named chairs, bought subscriptions, and contributed various amounts, giving our Hall the true imprimatur of community.

We opened Jazz at Lincoln Center's Frederick P. Rose Hall on October 18, 2004. In a touching tribute, our board chose this date as it was my birthday and, ironically, it was also the date our bassist Carlos Henriquez and his wife, Sarah, had their first child, Carlos. What a night! We were all overjoyed. We started in the afternoon with a New Orleans–style parade that ended in the Hall's echoey corridors. Among us was Geoff Ward, a connoisseur of jazz and one of America's greatest citizens.

OPPOSITE: Lisa Schiff, chairman of the board, announces the grand opening of the Frederick P. Rose Hall in 2004.

ABOVE, TOP: Ricky Gordon, washboard player, Dr. Michael White, clarinetist, Vince Giordano, sousaphonist, Bob Wilber, soprano saxophonist, Ron Westray, trombonist, Wynton Marsalis, trumpeter, Victor Goines, soprano saxophonist, and Bob Stewart parade down Broadway to the House of Swing on opening day in 2004.

ABOVE: Geoff and Diane Ward follow the grand opening parade to Jazz at Lincoln Center's new home in Time Warner Center in 2004.

GEOFFREY C. WARD
HISTORIAN

STANDING ON THE CORNER

of Sixtieth and Broadway with other happy second-liners singing "When the Saints," I suddenly heard an enormous velvety baritone just over my shoulder. It was Milt Grayson—dressed to the nines, as he always was—come to honor the new home that had been built for the music he'd already been making for five decades.

HOSPITALITY 97

SLIDE HAMPTON COMPOSED A FANFARE, and there were speeches and tributes. Congressman Jerry Nadler said that just as the House that (Babe) Ruth built was filled with homeruns, we'd have to make sure we fill this house with swing and great concerts. Igor Butman flew from Moscow to Vladivostok, through Seoul and Anchorage to New York, just to participate.

IGOR BUTMAN
SAXOPHONIST
IGOR BUTMAN QUARTET

HOW COULD I NOT COME OVER?

I was the sole representative of Russia and, generally speaking, overseas jazz. The success of Rose Hall proved that even the most bold and challenging projects can get off the ground, and the music of all the musicians who have appeared over the years has proven, better than words ever could, the need for jazz to have a house of its own. So now we face the daunting challenge of building these houses, or, in a broader sense, temples of jazz, everywhere. I hope we shall succeed in doing this in Moscow.

MUSICIANS, THE ORCHESTRA, AND THE PROGramming has always been our central focus. We ran the gamut that night from the Afro-Latin Orchestra with Arturo O'Farrill and special guest Paquito D'Rivera in the Allen Room, to Bill Charlap performing a set with his mother, Sandy Stewart, in Dizzy's Club, to the JLCO in the Rose Theater playing everything from Coltrane to Oliver Nelson and, then, playing with our mothers, fathers, and brothers. It was a celebration of the continuum from many angles. This continued for the next two weeks with a roster of great artists including Garth Fagan, Ricky Skaggs, Tony Bennett, Bill Cosby, Hermeto Pascoal, Savion Glover, Mark O'Connor, Randy Weston, and Toshiko Akiyoshi. The procession alone was powerful. After the festivities died down, all of Jazz at Lincoln Center was bone tired, but in the end, we knew that our efforts had changed, ever so slightly, the physical and cultural landscape of our country.

BILL CHARLAP
PIANIST

NEW YORK IS IN MY BLOOD.

I was born here and grew up here. I remember Columbus Circle in the days before Jazz at Lincoln Center. So now, when I look at Fifty-Ninth Street and Columbus Avenue, I'm filled with gratitude and awe. Smack dab in the middle of the city, the first complex of its kind, ever. A concert hall, an amphitheater, and a jazz club, all beautifully appointed, all state of the art, all devoted to the art form of jazz. It makes me proud to be a New Yorker.

OPPOSITE: The Afro-Latin Jazz Orchestra led by Arturo O'Farrill performs in the Allen Room as part of the grand opening festival in 2004.

AARON DIEHL WAS TWELVE years old when we started working our way toward the House of Swing. He would become a member of the artistic corps that undergirded its construction.

AARON DIEHL
PIANIST, FORMER ESSENTIALLY ELLINGTON PARTICIPANT

SINCE FREDERICK P. ROSE HALL OPENED

in 2004, I have had the fortune of playing in Dizzy's Club Coca-Cola, the Allen Room, Rose Theater, and plenty of background gigs where no one seemed to be listening. They listened enough to support the cause. This is proven by the rapid growth of the institution and, of course, the hard-working efforts of all those people determined to keep it thriving. It is vital that it continues, because the House of Swing is a meeting place—a confluence of the scene where uptown sits in with downtown, and musical alliances can be forged simply on the basis of serendipity.

RIGHT: JLCO performing at Frederick P. Rose Hall in 2006.

AT LISA'S FINAL BOARD MEETING AS CHAIRMAN, Gordon spoke with great emotion and respect about all that she had accomplished. Dizzy's Club was full of senior staff and board members. In conclusion, he said, "What we do is, and has always been, about the music." He then gave her a scroll with a listing of every concert we produced, presented, and played during her tenure. It was ten pages long.

Albert Murray always said that quality art is the key to our success and should command our focus and direction. And the standard is so high. It was set by Louis Armstrong and Duke Ellington, maintained by Art Tatum and Charlie Parker, rearticulated by Miles Davis and Charles Mingus, among other musicians who spent lifetimes of hours in practice rooms and on uncompromising bandstands battling to be the best, the most individual. From the outset, we were driven to rise to the level of this tradition, to compete with the best ever, and to stay inside the reality of our music: blues and swing. These are the pillars of Jazz at Lincoln Center and the fundamentals of our success.

I love our orchestra and feel privileged to have spent my adult life playing with them. We learn and play music of all styles and eras: New Orleans, bebop, avant-garde, our latest compositions, it doesn't matter. We respect it all. At first we were figuring it out, but now we have our own tradition of excellence. It's how we were trained to play and how we love to play. Indefatigable on the road and completely reliable, night after night, even under the most difficult circumstances and under the pressures of high-level performance. The cats are for real. Music, music, music. We even have ten arrangers!

PREVIOUS SPREAD: Hotel Bar at Ritz Carlton, Berlin.

OPPOSITE, TOP: The grand reunion of the Wynton Marsalis Septet at Dizzy's Club Coca-Cola in 2007. From left to right: Wynton Marsalis, Marcus Roberts, pianist, Todd Williams, tenor saxophonist, Wycliffe Gordon, trombonist, Herlin Riley, drummer, and Reginald Veal, bassist.

OPPOSITE, BOTTOM: Herlin Riley, drummer, in 2004.

HERLIN RILEY
FORMER DRUMMER
JAZZ AT LINCOLN CENTER ORCHESTRA

I WAS A MEMBER OF THE WYNTON MARSALIS SEPTET,

and the members of the septet eventually became members of the LCJO. I was honored to be the first drummer to tour with the orchestra in 1992, and continued until 2005. In the early days, we mainly played Duke Ellington's compositions. Some members of the first orchestra were seasoned veterans who had played in Duke's orchestra. These men took as much pride in rehearsing as in performing. At all times, they played with passion and intensity. They were colorful personalities too!

Trombonist Britt Woodman, who would have been seventy-three at the time, had a narcoleptic condition and would fall asleep in the middle of the card games on the bus, only to wake up a few minutes later, fresh as a daisy, to play out his hand. Lead alto saxophonist Norris Turney, seventy-two, would invite you to an "eye opener" (a shot of vodka) while traveling through an airport at 7 A.M. One day in rehearsal, trumpeter and Detroit legend Marcus Belgrave, sixty-two, threatened to pull out his knife and cut the so-called "barracuda" that had supposedly stolen his mouthpiece. There was a ruckus, but the mouthpiece turned up in his trumpet case, and no blood was shed.

Milt Grayson, sixty-two, kept a do-rag/stocking cap on all day long to keep his "process" hairdo in place. He also made sure to polish his cowboy boots so he looked as good as he sounded. And then there is Joe Temperley, a man of eighty-plus years and the only original member besides Wynton who's still swinging and holding down the baritone sax chair. Whenever the bus would hit a bump in the road, Joe would shout, "Put the round wheels on the bus!"

METHODOLOGY

LEFT: JLCO encore for "C Jam Blues" in Santa Rosa, California, in 2008. Marcus Printup, trumpeter, is on the right.

MARCUS PRINTUP
TRUMPETER
JAZZ AT LINCOLN CENTER ORCHESTRA

THERE WAS A PARTY at David Ostwald's home around 1996. I remember there being a jam session. I played a few tunes and noticed that the great trombonist Al Grey walked into the room. I didn't know him well at the time but of course admired his work. Maybe a half an hour went by and he felt compelled to grace us with some words of wisdom. He was so moved that jazz music was in a great resurgence, and the home jam sessions reminded him of the 1950s. He then said, "When I first walked in, I knew the trumpet player was Marcus Printup because he has his own sound." I didn't even know he knew my name! Hearing those words from this man changed my life. God bless you, Mr. Grey.

ABOVE: Ted Nash, woodwind musician, and Walter Blanding, clarinetist, backstage in 2001.

ABOVE, RIGHT: JLCO performance in front of Picasso's *Les Demoiselles d'Avignon* at Rose Hall.

TED NASH
WOODWIND MUSICIAN
JAZZ AT LINCOLN CENTER
ORCHESTRA

WHEN ASKED TO COMPOSE a long-form

piece for the band, I decided to dedicate each movement to a different iconic painter. We collaborated with the Museum of Modern Art, whose rich collection and love and support of jazz made it a perfect relationship. The museum allowed me to visit during off-hours to enjoy the artworks with very little distraction. Once I brought my soprano sax and played in front of Picasso's *Les Demoiselles d'Avignon.* As the last sound reverberated, I glanced over to the doorway; there stood a security guard, smiling and nodding his head.

AT AROUND FIFTEEN YEARS OLD,

I was exposed to the best thing that had ever happened to me: the Jazz at Lincoln Center Orchestra. I was introduced to them by my friend Steven Oquendo, trumpeter in my high school jazz band. He told me that the orchestra's rehearsals were always open for younger musicians. I knew then that the opportunity to be with great jazz musicians was near. Just sitting through these rehearsals was essential to my development as a musician and was also instructive in learning how to deal with other people. Even though I was only fifteen years old, Wynton knew if I had knowledge on a topic. He would occasionally ask me for advice on Latin rhythms. This would freak me out because I was surrounded by the best of jazz, but hearing my young self talk about Latin music was kind of hip.

The orchestra would bust their behinds getting music prepared—with very little time. In spite of this pressure, they were humble to everyone around them. I remember how much love every member gave me as a high school student! Not once did I ever feel unwanted. Now, having been a part of the JLCO for twelve years, I continue this same tradition for our next generation.

CARLOS HENRIQUEZ
BASSIST
JAZZ AT LINCOLN CENTER ORCHESTRA

RIGHT: Carlos Henriquez Jr. tries Ali Jackson's drums as Walter Blanding, his father Carlos, Susan John, and Vincent Gardner observe.

FAR RIGHT: Carlos Henriquez performing at the Arvada Center in Arvada, Colorado, in 2011.

IN ORDER TO REHEARSE, YOU MUST HAVE music. Kay Niewood and our music preparation team do the impossible on a regular basis.

BELOW: Drummers Jason Marsalis and Ali Jackson, and the mighty JLCO trumpet section with Wynton Marsalis, Ryan Kisor, Kenny Rampton, and Marcus Printup performing at Frederick P. Rose Hall in 2010.

BELOW, BOTTOM: Saxophonists Joe Temperley, Sherman Irby, Ted Nash, and Victor Goines performing in Santa Barbara, California, in 2009.

KAY NIEWOOD
DIRECTOR, JAZZ LIBRARY
JAZZ AT LINCOLN CENTER

ANY WEEK IS CRAZY WEEK.

This is typical: The JLCO has just finished a tour, and ten of the JLCO members are arranging music for this week's concert. We only have three of the new charts by Saturday morning. Four more charts come in by Sunday night. The first day of rehearsal, we are still missing three charts. Ali Jackson shows up with his chart on his laptop. Victor Goines finishes his at the break but has PDFs so we can play it right away. The second day of rehearsal, Ali sends a new version of his charts at eight o'clock in the morning, and Walter Blanding has just arrived with the last of his arrangement on a flash drive. I open it and a score is the only thing there. Christi English is busy dealing with changes that are needed on the charts they are rehearsing right now. Jonathan Kelly, Austin Harris, and I have been up half the night engraving music. Maybe Geoff Burke or Kate Sain will be awake to finish Walter's chart before the afternoon rehearsal.

ABOVE: Rodney Whitaker, double bassist, and Marcus Roberts, pianist, in 1997.

RIGHT: The march offstage after a concert in 2000.

RIGHT: Wycliffe Gordon with his trombone.

BELOW: Double bassist Rodney Whitaker exiting the stage after a performance in 2002.

THE ROAD IS ABOUT CONQUERING A SERIES OF unforeseen challenges and hitting the stage on time. We had a road manager, Billy Banks, who spoke four languages and knew more about the music than we did.

BILLY BANKS
PRODUCTION MANAGER
JAZZ AT LINCOLN CENTER

THIS IS A FACTUAL ACCOUNT

of a three-day touring period a few years ago. The orchestra was touring Europe, about twenty people, orchestra and support staff, riding on two tour buses with an equipment truck. All was going extremely well. Next stop: Cologne, Germany. We arrived a day before our performance, and saxophonist Wess Anderson took ill saying it was the worst he had ever felt. I got him to an emergency room. They admitted him for further observation. The same day, saxophonist Joe Temperley had a severely abscessed wisdom tooth and a high fever. I sat with him in a dental office until it got fixed.

Wess missed the concert. And although the Cologne concert went well, I was anxious to get to Munich for the next evening's performance. I scheduled a morning departure for our buses and settled down to get some much-needed rest. Around 3 A.M, I am awakened with a call. The second bus had broken down and was in no shape to go to Munich. Space on the first bus was limited, and there was no time to locate a new bus. I got on the phone and was able to get six or seven tickets on a flight that would get the second bus's passengers to Munich on schedule. The equipment truck had left, so I jammed the excess luggage on the first bus and off we went to Munich.

The first bus and the airline travelers arrived at the hotel in Munich around the same time, and even before we opened the luggage bay of the bus, I sensed something was wrong. Because some of the added luggage pushed against a light switch when the bay door was closed, three or four bulbs didn't turn off and the lights had burned through several pieces of luggage and clothing (mine included). The whole bay was filled with smoke, and we were lucky the entire bus hadn't gone up in flames. I spent the rest of the day getting the band onstage, forcing the presenter to change our hotel, and getting Wess to a hospital, where he was diagnosed with and began treatment for diabetes. The next day was a day off in Munich, and I spent it shopping for clothes and locating a bus for the rest of the tour—not an easy feat during the height of touring season in Europe. We found a good one and headed down the Good King's highway. Next time, I'll tell you about the time when we got to New Orleans for JazzFest; it was ninety degrees with 90 percent humidity, and we discovered that our pianist, Marcus Roberts, had come down with chicken pox.

ABOVE: Trumpeter Marcus Belgrave (left), sound engineer David Robinson, trombonist Wycliffe Gordon, and Wynton Marsalis backstage at Belgrave's birthday performance in 1992.

RIGHT: Joe.

OPPOSITE: David Robinson, sound engineer, and Billy Banks, production manager, inside the tour bus.

LEFT: Trombonists Chris Crenshaw and Vincent Gardner going onstage in 2009.

ABOVE, TOP: Trombonists Vincent Gardner and Chris Crenshaw leaving the stage after a 2008 concert in Mesa, Arizona.

ABOVE: Portrait of Joe Wilder.

OPPOSITE: Milt Grayson.

CHRIS CRENSHAW
TROMBONIST
JAZZ AT LINCOLN CENTER
ORCHESTRA

I REMEMBER WYNTON

talking to me while he was shooting hoops in the rehearsal studio. This was after we played at Essentially Ellington in May of 2006. I wasn't in the band yet, but he pointed out my attributes after a couple of times sitting in. He'd make a shot. "You're serious." Another shot would go in. "You're soulful." One more southpaw jumper. "You're country." He kept going on and on, and he couldn't miss, on either front. The last compliment he said was, "You're honest. I hear that honesty in your playing, son. That will take you a long way. It will help you be yourself. You have a lot to offer." I needed that shot in the arm after wondering how life would get better for me in New York City. A month later, I joined the JLCO, a band I had been keeping up with since high school, with my cousins and friends, the same cousins and friends who told me about Wynton's jumper. I experienced that jumper face-to-face once in Louisville, Kentucky, at a sound check in 2007, but that was after he witnessed mine face-to-face. Draws!

ONE OF THE MAIN THINGS WE TEACH OUR NEW members is work ethic. On the stage it is a given, but David Robinson, our sound man for all these years, sets the lights, stage, and does sound for the show. He works all day and all night at every gig. He is the orchestra's sixteenth man.

DAVID ROBINSON
SOUND ENGINEER
JAZZ AT LINCOLN CENTER

FROM THE FIRST TOUR WITH THE ELLINGTON ALUMNI,

the die was cast. To hear Mr. Joe Wilder stand up on his one solo of the night and play the trumpet derby with the touch and taste of a true master was an absolute joy. To see Milt Grayson glide onstage in those black cowboy boots and slicked-back hair and sing "Multi-Colored Blue" so sweet you'd want to cry. To watch Sir Roland Hanna practice his Chopin études every day as I set the bandstand for sound check, and later hear him drive the band through the book of Ellington that night, just swinging away. To hear Norris Turney play "Jeep's Blues"—his way.

True enough, there have been bumps along the way. But it was always about the music. Like the time in Germany I got nose-to-nose with my buddy Farid Barron about where the piano should be placed. Or the nightly go-round with Cassandra Wilson about her monitor during *Blood on the Fields*. She swore I was sabotaging her. But hey, I didn't have the slightest idea about monitor engineering! We got through it and I got a new sobriquet courtesy of her: Celebrity Sound Man!

Words can't express how good it feels at afternoon sound check when fifteen of the finest musicians holding instruments are in place, and our esteemed leader sits down in the trumpet section, and says, "What you need, Hoon?" Man, I already got it. The honor of hearing this music every night for nearly half of my life.

MARCUS PRINTUP
TRUMPETER
JAZZ AT LINCOLN CENTER
ORCHESTRA

WE LEFT FOR A WEST COAST TOUR

on September 8, 2001. We were rehearsing *All Rise* with the Los Angeles Philharmonic. Three days later, my phone rang at 7 A.M. It was Wynton calling to tell me to turn on the television and check out what's happening in New York City. I asked which channel? He replied, "Any channel." I feel blessed to have been with my brothers during this difficult time. The band, orchestra, and choir came together musically and spiritually during this week. We performed the first major outdoor concert after the tragedy at the Hollywood Bowl a few days later.

When the Los Angeles Philharmonic played the national anthem, all of the cats in our band stood up and played along, and I remember tears streaming down many of our faces. After Los Angeles, our next stop was in Seattle. We drove, as all flights were canceled. A member of the L.A. Philharmonic brought blankets for the entire band. We drove twenty-one hours straight to Seattle. The bus pulled in at 8:15 P.M. for an eight o'clock show. We came straight off the bus (sweaty, funky!), got dressed, and *played!* We opened with the "The Stars and Stripes Forever" and the people embraced us as never before.

ABOVE: Susan John, former director of touring.

ABOVE, RIGHT: Kenny Rampton, trumpeter, and Victor Goines going over the music before their show in Gardone Riviera, Italy, in 2011.

OPPOSITE: JLCO going onstage to perform in Virginia Beach, Virginia, in 2009.

RAYMOND MURPHY
TOUR MANAGER
JAZZ AT LINCOLN CENTER

WE WERE IN LOS ANGELES the week of September 11, 2001,

rehearsing and recording *All Rise*. On September 12, rehearsals began, although it was difficult for everyone to focus. After a full day of rehearsal, our tour manager, Nathan George, approached me and said, "I need you and Eric Wright [then our production assistant] to go to Colorado Springs [1,170 miles away, a 17-hour drive] and pick up the Sony producer Steve Epstein." My reply was, "Sure, when do we need to leave?" Nate replied, "Right now. I need him here Thursday at 10 A.M., when the recording starts." Averaging a speed of ninety miles per hour, Eric and I completed the mission with three hours to spare.

ABOVE: Pianist Dan Nimmer reading music scores in 2008.

OPPOSITE: Esa-Pekka Salonen conducts *All Rise* at the Hollywood Bowl in 2001.

DAN NIMMER
PIANIST
JAZZ AT LINCOLN CENTER
ORCHESTRA

WHEN I WAS GROWING UP, my parents used

to take me to hear the Milwaukee Symphony Orchestra. I always wondered what it would sound like and feel like to be onstage with all of those musicians. On my first tour with the band in 2005, we performed *All Rise* with the London Philharmonic Orchestra. To be surrounded by all of that powerful and acoustic sound, rendered by so many virtuosic musicians in a magnificent concert hall, is something you have to experience for yourself in order to understand how truly great it is. And then you had the guys in our band coming together with the philharmonic orchestra to make a seamless connection. It was beautiful. This set the tone for all of the great moments and memories I have experienced, playing with my brothers in the band.

TED NASH
WOODWIND MUSICIAN
JAZZ AT LINCOLN CENTER ORCHESTRA

MANY OF US HAVE PARENTS AND SIBLINGS

who are great musicians, and whenever we have the opportunity, we invite them to be part of our music. Vincent Gardner, Ryan Kisor, Walter Blanding, Elliot Mason, Wynton, Wycliffe "Cone" Gordon, Wessell "Warmdaddy" Anderson, and I have all had a family member play with us at some point, and it is always a special occasion. A few years back, the band was performing in California at the Cerritos Center for the Performing Arts, and my father, Dick, drove down from Los Angeles with my mother to hear the concert. I told my dad to bring his trombone, just in case. During the second set, Wynton, aware of my father's presence, made a heartwarming speech about family and invited my father to come join us. All of a sudden, we see a man in his late seventies literally jogging up the aisle and on to the stage, his horn in hand ready for business. Without a moment's hesitation, he said, "Blues! In C. One, two, one, two, three, four..."

ABOVE, LEFT: Father and son, Dick and Ted Nash, perform in Los Angeles in 2011.

ABOVE: Walter Blanding plays solo while Vincent Gardner looks on.

OPPOSITE: Wynton Marsalis and the rhythm section play an encore with an unscripted second line at the 2009 New Orleans Jazz and Heritage Festival.

ALI JACKSON
DRUMMER
JAZZ AT LINCOLN CENTER ORCHESTRA

THE JLCO AND ODADAA! WERE REHEARSING

Congo Square in April of 2009. Because of spring break, many of us had our children at these rehearsals. The ages of the kids ranged from toddlers to teenagers. The vibe of the music and the children's activity made it a memorable moment. It was a real "village." Many of the guys in the band were sharing music and life experiences with each other's kids. Some kids were getting tutored in math by Victor Goines. Other kids were getting a saxophone lesson with Walter Blanding. Some kids were drawing pictures of the JLCO. My son Aziel was juggling a soccer ball through the rehearsal. On the breaks, our senior member, Joe Temperley, kicked the ball around with him, while Oni, Wynton's daughter, was checking out the music and crawling around. This encapsulates so many soulful days of rehearsal with the JLCO.

TOP, LEFT: Wynton Marsalis Jr. plays under his father's chair.

TOP, CENTER: Drummer Ali Jackson with his two sons, Aziel (front) and Tamian (right), in 2004.

TOP, RIGHT: Jazzline Crenshaw plays with her father Chris's trombone.

ABOVE: Ali Jackson plays a drum solo during a JLCO performance in Santa Barbara, California, in 2009.

LEFT: Ron Westray, Wess "Warmdaddy" Anderson, Herlin Riley, Wynton Marsalis, Victor Goines, and Andre Hayward play a second-line parade in Yokohama, Japan, in 2002.

SINCE 1992, JAZZ AT LINCOLN CENTER ORCHESTRA HAS played in 425 cities in thirty-seven countries on six continents. From 2005 to 2012, we produced *The Rhythm Road: American Music Abroad* with the U.S. Department of State's Bureau of Educational and Cultural Affairs. In six years, we sent 180 musicians, from forty-six ensembles, to visit 116 different countries, on five continents. Our touring director, Susan John, came to jazz through her family. Her father loved jazz and the *New York Times*, and she experienced a lot of the world on the road with us.

SUSAN JOHN
FORMER DIRECTOR OF TOURING
JAZZ AT LINCOLN CENTER

HUMANS ALL OVER THE WORLD

do similar things with some differences. In Italy, their costumes are stylish; in Singapore, their streets are fastidiously clean; in Sri Lanka, the signposts are in Sinhalese, whose script conjures sleeping puppies; in Birmingham, you will be reminded to look right by kindly pavements accustomed to Americans surveying the wrong side of the road before crossing; in Spain, the meals are long and pour from every door; in Havana, they are more precious and no less succulent; in Scotland, the twilight, or the gloaming, as they say, will pierce your very core; in Kuala Lumpur, the Petronas Towers will raise your eyes and spirit to the heights that Gothic spires may once have mounted.

I came for the music, jazz music, and learned more than I could fathom. I learned how I'd like to be loved from Wess Anderson's version of "Isfahan"; how I'd like life to be paced from Sherman Irby's rendition of "Blues Walk"; how joy is boundless if you find yourself the right chair (or throne, as it is aptly named) from Herlin Riley; how mythology is timeless and cyclical, for Ryan Kisor is Apollo; how sound can be a blanket and a mountain; and proof that the world is good from Walter Blanding. I came for the music but I stayed for the people, dozens of whom never graced the bandstand but quietly carried it on their shoulders. To these spirits and musicians alike, I am grateful.

LEFT: Herlin Riley, tambourine man, in 2003.

WE ALWAYS HAVE JOE PLAY AT OR NEAR
the end of pieces so that they have a happy ending.

JOE TEMPERLEY
SAXOPHONIST
JAZZ AT LINCOLN CENTER
ORCHESTRA

FROM ALICE TULLY HALL TO ROSE HALL

and the entire world in between. Buses, planes, trains, all the travel. The thrill of playing every night with this wonderful group of musicians. I look forward to it, disregarding the rigors of travel. I have always felt thankful being a part of it. We play for people from every walk of life. The love and respect that is returned to us from all over the world playing the music of Ellington, Gillespie, Coltrane, Parker; Spanish, Cuban, African music; and some good old swinging jazz. Watching and participating in the growth and excitement of the young people playing jazz is so rewarding, knowing we put it out there for them.

Most of all, Jazz at Lincoln Center Orchestra has remained consistent since the very beginning in the truest sense of family and brotherhood. Thank you, Wynton, for the soulful, inspirational playing at every performance; and thank you, Ted Nash, Chris Crenshaw, and Sherman Irby for writing such beautiful music for me to play.

RIGHT: Joe Temperley at the Teatro Romano in Aosta, Italy, in 2011.

WEALTH

JALC'S GREATEST ASSET IS THE COLLECTIVE LABOR OF EVERYONE WHO WORKS on behalf of our mission. But an institution is defined and guided by its highest level of leadership. Of all the theoretical ideas—and in jazz there are many—the concept of a volunteer board has got to be the most abstract. Being raised the son of a jazz musician, the thought that a group of citizens would champion jazz as a cause, become evangelical about it, establish the direction and mission for it, regularly debate the meaning of that mission, open their homes for receptions and other events, provide and cultivate economic resources to develop and maintain programs, travel around the world at a moment's notice to support initiatives, and attend a steady diet of meetings was beyond what could be dreamed.

When Gordon held those first seminal meetings before we developed the board, I thought, "How long will this last? No one ever gives anything to jazz but grief." To this moment, I am astounded by the dedication and pride of our board. Of course, we have all the typical dysfunctions that all familial-type situations proudly offer, but, when it's time to come together—we come strong!

In April 2012, we welcomed a new chairman to steer us into our twenty-fifth year—Robert Appel. Bob is dedicated to seeing jazz occupy its richly deserved position at the forefront of global culture. As Lisa Schiff says, "His desire to perpetuate the democratic spirit of America's music in our New York home and around the world is infectious."

ROBERT APPEL
CHAIRMAN
JAZZ AT LINCOLN CENTER

MY PERSONAL EXPERIENCE

started with a passionate and almost instinctive love of jazz music at a young age—and the idolization of those who played it. I caught lots of shows. I learned how to play a little bit. No doubt, aspects of this music informed me in many subtle ways as I went out into the world as an investor and, later, a philanthropist. From the first time I connected with JALC some ten years ago, I knew I had to be involved and sought a quick and complete immersion into the organization. I am so thankful to the founding members for bringing quality jazz to us and for creating, through their incredibly hard work and perseverance, this wonderful institution to preserve and memorialize it. JALC's product is extraordinary, our mission is clear, and we have an enviable record in attracting private philanthropy. The great challenge now is to grow our audience and to allow many others to have, for the first time, the profound experience that this music can engender. Two examples bring this home: a concert my wife and I promoted at Cornell University in 2010 and a major private event in 2012. In both instances, the orchestra was extremely well received by two large audiences. By my count, more than half present had never heard the JALC orchestra swing and do its thing. They were awestruck and outspoken in their profound appreciation for that sublime sense of joy that's difficult to describe but "you know when you feel it." These new converts and other groups like them most certainly contain some of the audiences and supporters of the future, and it is my job and that of other trustees to find them, turn them on to the music, and bring them into the great legacy of JALC.

PREVIOUS SPREAD: Board members thanking Lisa Schiff as she steps down as chairman of the board, 2012.

ABOVE: Helen and Robert Appel, 2008.

OPPOSITE, TOP: Todd Barkan, Dion Parson, and The 21st Century Band getting ready for a show.

OPPOSITE, BOTTOM: Arlise Ganaway-Ellis at the press desk, 2009.

WEALTH 131

JALC BOARD OF DIRECTORS AND FRIENDS

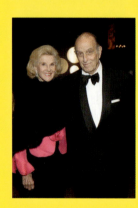

132 JAZZ AT LINCOLN CENTER

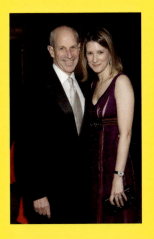

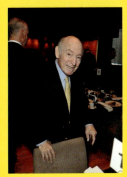

WEALTH 133

COUNTDOWN TO SHOWTIME

JALC PRODUCES AND PRESENTS CONCERTS WITH THE JLCO AND other ensembles of various shapes and sizes. Whether rehearsing for a performance, teaching young people of all ages, preparing to take our show on the road, or opening our doors to a rental client, there is something happening in the House of Swing every day and every night of the year. And making it happen is all about the staff.

EIGHTEEN MONTHS OR MORE

In our programming department, Phil Schaap, Todd Barkan, Jason Olaine, and I argue over what and who to program, where and when. Sometimes we go through all twentysomething years of programming, concert by concert, just to make a point. We consider a variety of factors, chief among them what we should add to the library. Let's give Kay Niewood, the manager of it, something good.

Say we decide to do a concert with the JLCO and special guests called Nursery Song Swing. Some think it's a dumb idea, but we agreed long ago not to take credit for great shows, or place blame for the bad ones. After we commit to a concept, it goes to the staff for the when and how.

Cat Henry, executive producer, sets aside the possible dates, contracts the guest artists, and ensures that there is a business agreement. Producer Eric Wright assesses the technical requirements.

The basic artist contract has been issued by the legal department. James Grooms, general counsel, makes sure that we are on the right side of any possible legal issues. Jae K. Lee has established the standards for contracting artists, and after Daphnée Saget Woodley has acquired all rights and clearances for the performance, the contract template is good to go.

Dwayne Ashley, chief officer of development, is responsible for raising money to support our programs and operations. Nursery Song Swing provides an easy entry into the world of JALC. His team is all over this.

Sarah Haberman thinks that many on her list of individual donors would enjoy hearing a jazz version of "Old MacDonald." She will bring some of them to the rehearsals. Roslyn Turner knows that her members will support this with full force, while Lauren Arana makes sure the board has it on their calendars.

This concert aligns with one of Kaitlyn Falk Wong's grant proposals to fund children-friendly concerts. She is always looking for any foundation or government agency that would even remotely fund jazz programming, while Katie Lander searches for music lovers who could support concerts or programming in general.

Gabrielle Armand, director of corporate sponsorships, begins talking to our corporate partners. She has a variety of ways to offer their customers special access to this newly arranged material. She also works on a strategy to interest companies who may want to sponsor a family event or distribute a recording of this concert.

ONE YEAR TO NINE MONTHS

Once the concert is scheduled, it's up to Jon Yanofsky, director of marketing, to decide how to reach audiences by delivering our message through advertising and branding. Every step in the lead-up to this concert will receive detailed attention from his entire team.

Before the brochure or any advertisements go out, the creative services team, led by Luis Bravo, will design the artwork and marketing materials. They give Jon's marketing language a graphic identity. Casey Walter, Ho-Mui Wong, and Maya Sariahmed work with Luis to create poster layouts, collateral materials, and ads that reflect our brand spirit. They strive to grab people's attention and make them think, "That looks like something we shouldn't miss."

Their design work goes back to Jon's team, where Sara Lalli will make sure all advertisements are submitted and running at the appropriate time. After tickets go on sale, she will monitor those sales to ensure as many people as possible will be in attendance by concert time. Orin Chait and Karen Reeves send out reminder emails to all our ticket holders, chase down any ticketing loose ends, both internally and externally, in coordination with the box office. Orin also sends out a weekly ticket report. Nicole Lumpress creates and manages all of our social media posts to help build the excitement, while Andy McGibbon makes sure that specific information on this gig is prominently displayed throughout the website.

SIX TO THREE MONTHS

The public relations team led, by Mary Fiance, is ready to help get the word out.

Mary pitches hard-copy magazines and television shows about the overall JLCO season. And Zooey Jones will pitch local press for previews in media outlets. She will also try to get the show reviewed and will schedule the orchestra members' interviews with the press.

As the fundraising and marketing continues, Arlise Ellis in the sales and scheduling department of Frederick P. Rose Hall has confirmed Cat's dates, and the Hall starts rolling.

Depending on who gets assigned the gig, David Taylor, John Starmer, or Michael Givey from the production department in the Hall communicates with the concert's line producer, Eric Wright, to understand what he needs from them.

The Hall production manager, Michael Leslie, determines the number of stage crew and type of equipment required. He gives Julia Graham enough information to estimate how much all of that will cost.

Back in Cat's world of production and concert administration, Jennie Wasserman reviews the press release and marketing copy to make sure that descriptions of Nursery Song Swing accurately reflect the program and personnel.

Kris Kandel reserves and manages the Hall spaces we need for rehearsals and performances. Sometimes, more important, he assigns the dressing rooms.

Eric Wright communicates with various Hall managers to determine lighting, sound, and stage crew needs.

Cat makes sure the stage manager, Billy Banks; sound engineer, David Robinson; recording engineer, James Nichols; and artist assistant, Jay Sgroi are contracted or assigned. And then she provides information about the artists and program for the concert playbill, which she will approve before it's printed.

THREE MONTHS TO ONE MONTH

I have asked eight of our ten arrangers in the orchestra to choose their favorite nursery rhyme and send the tune, tempo, groove, and key to our associate director of music administration, Kay Niewood. She makes suggestions for appropriate songs that may be in the library, and Christi English will track down all the original sheet music and recordings for the arrangers. All contracting of arrangers, transcribers, and music copyists—Kay will handle it. She begins to check off what is done and needs to be done. Then I get the list and put the show in order, determining which songs go where, and when the special guests will appear.

Everyone is managing costs and making sure the concert stays within our budget, but Josué Urbina in development manages the database of gifts and is always on the lookout for sources of contributed income that may help defray some of those costs.

Naeemah Hicks has booked all the necessary transportation, hotels, and equipment months ago. Now the performance is only a week away. The orchestra and guests have assembled to rehearse. I called Kay last night to make sure we were ready, and during the course of our conversation, realized I forgot to do one arrangement. One more sleepless night for music copyist Jonathan Kelly.

Eric Wright attends rehearsals and monitors the content, length, and flow of the show. He makes sure the musicians are on the same page with the production team and keeps everyone on time. (Not easy.)

Kay and Christi shuttle between the rehearsals and the office making corrections to music where needed. Austin Harris and Grace Parisi round out the team that engraves, prints, and copies music that is then taped into parts and put into named folders: "Kenny Rampton 2nd Trumpet JLCO."

ONE WEEK

We rush to learn thirteen new original arrangements, and there are always kids and extra folks in rehearsal. We are all working on different sections of an arrangement at the same time, and kids and staff are running around for different reasons. It seems like pandemonium but, in the end, it will come together, if only because it always has and always does.

TWELVE HOURS

Thursday is finally here. The orchestra has many cues to remember and some difficult parts that will require a lot of concentration under the pressure of performance, but we are ready.

Early on the day of the show, Gabrielle, Mary Beth McGee, and Jenna Presto make sure that all of the corporate partners attending the show have their tickets, and that any special arrangements, like a separate check-in line or guest passes to the hospitality lounge, have been considered and are ready to roll.

FOUR HOURS

Mary Beth and Jenna go over to the Hall early to set up the MasterCard patrons' lounge so our supporters can enjoy complimentary refreshments or a comfortable place to sit and fellowship.

Darian Suggs makes sure that our board members and generous donors have their tickets to the concert and helps them with special requests.

TWO HOURS

Doug Hosney's team in the Hall is ready. Before anyone arrives, Ken Luciano and his team have set up and cleaned the lobbies. At the same time that Zak Al-Alami is working with Phil Hirsch and Scott Schilk to finalize the lighting look, Bobby Somerville, John Healey, Bob Biasetti, and John Uhl have prepared the stage; set up platforms, chairs, and stands; and focused the stage lighting, while others have put microphones in their proper place. They have tracked every change of set, so that transitions onstage will go smoothly.

Mary will coordinate the news crews on-site and Scott will work with the photographers.

Zooey is also in the Hall to make sure that all backstage photos and interviews go as planned. So is Lamont Johnson. He is making sure that press tickets are in place.

Rachel LeFevre-Snee is on hand to manage our preconcert activities such as artists' discussions and free music in the atrium. Her colleagues in the marketing department, Orin Chait and Karen Reeves, are seated next to the escalators, at the subscribers' table, to handle any and all ticketing needs.

ONE HOUR

Naeemah is making last checks with Bob Auer's front-of-house team on start time, intermission time, and preshow activities in the lobby.

Stacie Middleton Crawford is preparing to give our concert partners a glimpse of the backstage experience by organizing a meet-and-greet with the orchestra and me.

Jennie Wasserman makes sure the guest lists and complimentary tickets are where they should be, as well as the backstage hospitality for all musicians.

FIFTEEN MINUTES

David Robinson is at the soundboard, the orchestra is backstage warming up, and I am looking over my trumpet parts one more time.

As our guests arrive, Vincent Bly and the box office staff are selling tickets. House managers Nick Adler and Indio Melendez lead a team of ushers who guides everyone to their seats to get ready to start the show.

ERNIE GREGORY TELLS ME, "SHOWTIME, SHOWTIME!"

Suddenly, I'm past stage manager Billy Banks with the cats, and we're on the stage.

Good evening ladies and gentleman, welcome to the House of Swing. We are the Jazz at Lincoln Center Orchestra. Tonight we'd like to start with Ted Nash's arrangement of "Old MacDonald Had a Farm." We hope you enjoy it.

RIGHT: JLCO performing at the Frederick P. Rose Hall in 2007.

WHEN ALL IS SAID AND ALL IS DONE, WE AT JAZZ AT LINCOLN CENTER ARE HERE to lift our audience. We exist to serve and bring folks together. "To serve is to be served": That's what my manager, Ed Arrendell, always says.

And people in our neighborhood see us as a community organization. Our stagehands in Rose and Alice Tully Halls always embraced that feeling too. The crew in Alice Tully—Frank Farrante, Bobby Jacobi, and Artie Connaughton—saved me on many a night and took care of my young kids, let them watch and play games backstage. We would share food and good coffee. Those were great times.

But when we played badly, watch out! I've had cab drivers complain to me saying, "I should charge you double fare for that high ticket price." Our first year in the Hall, we programmed all kinds of collaborations and original compositions that people were lukewarm about, if not stone cold. When we got to May 19, 2005's, *The Swinging Music of Thad Jones* with Vincent Gardner as music director, people in our audience stood up and shouted, "Hallelujah! Finally some four-four swing in the House of Swing."

Since 1995, Geoff and Diane Ward have been coming to everything from young people's concerts to jam sessions. Geoff also volunteers to write the interspersed biographical script that is a definitive feature of our Hall of Fame concerts.

GEOFF WARD
HISTORIAN

ONE OF THE BLESSINGS

of being even peripherally connected with Jazz at Lincoln Center is the chance to brush shoulders with musicians whose power to move people has magic in it. Talking with John Lewis not long after he conducted what turned out to be his last concert, I asked him for his definition of jazz. No matter what form it takes, he said, it has to contain three elements: swing, or the suggestion of swing; surprise; and the eternal search for the blues.

I don't know of a better definition. Or a clearer statement of what Jazz at Lincoln Center exemplifies.

And just as John Lewis knew they would be, the blues has been found everywhere at Jazz at Lincoln Center—in the hair-raising flamenco passion of Chano Dominguez and the intricate West African rhythms of Yacub Addy and Odadaa!, in the dazzling country fiddling of Mark O'Connor, and in the Texas drawl of Willie Nelson—and in Wynton's own apartment, where, during one wee-small-hours encounter, Igor Butman from St. Petersburg, Russia, and Wynton Marsalis from Kenner, Louisiana, rediscovered and reexplored jazz music's common ground while we and three or four other lucky listeners hung on every soulful note.

Late one evening not long ago, Diane and I were in Dizzy's with our friend Jackie Harris. Phoebe Jacobs, an essential member of the greater Jazz at Lincoln Center family, had just died, and I think all three of us were looking to blues music for the kind of solace only it can bring. Herlin Riley, the irresistible personification of New Orleans swing, was leading a group that included the too-rarely-heard tenor player Todd Williams. During the second set, Victor Goines brushed past our table, carrying his horn and looking, he said he wanted "a piece of that." He got one—and the fierce but loving battle between the two that followed raised the temperature in the club by about fifty degrees. While we were still applauding, Jackie leaned over to Diane and asked if she thought we'd ever be lucky enough to hear anything like that again.

"Of course we will," she answered, and because of all that we've been privileged to witness at Jazz at Lincoln Center over the last quarter of a century, I know she was right.

PREVIOUS SPREAD: *Higher Ground* second line, Frederick P. Rose Hall, 2005.

OPPOSITE, TOP: Swing dance at The Supper Club.

OPPOSITE, BOTTOM: The 2000 *For Dancers Only* tour with the JLCO. Paolo Lanna and Janice Wilson tear up the stage.

ABOVE: Wynton Marsalis encore.
OPPOSITE: Dianne Reeves, 2009.

DIZZY'S CLUB COCA-COLA HAS BEEN the hub of our activities in the House of Swing, and with a new club opening in Doha, Qatar, in October 2012, it will be an outpost for Lincoln Center, the first permanent home for any constituent outside the United States. Todd Barkan has been the voice of jazz at Dizzy's since we opened.

TODD BARKAN
ARTISTIC DIRECTOR
DIZZY'S CLUB COCA-COLA
JAZZ AT LINCOLN CENTER

IN OUR SENSORIALLY BOMBARDED WORLD,

it's easy to maintain an enthusiasm for something for twenty-five minutes, or even for twenty-five days, but when we see totally dedicated men and women producing and sharing inspirational jazz music for ten, twenty-five, fifty, and more years, then we begin to understand and appreciate the core effort of the magic and the miracle we're truly blessed to experience.

Dizzy's is all about consistently maintaining a warm and welcoming environment conducive to musical storytelling.

In a very integral way, it serves as the front porch and parlor of our Hall, helping make it more and more of a House of Love for the music itself.

THE GREATEST PERFORMANCE WITNESSED BY THE ORCHESTRA in Rose Theater was delivered on February 19, 2009, by Dianne Reeves. She sang "Misty" with such spontaneity, clarity, and depth that we and the audience erupted in a thunderous ovation then sat in stunned ecstasy for a long interval after the applause. A native of Denver, Ms. Reeves once came to our concert there and sat in the trumpet section for the whole second half, had the entire band out to the house, and cooked a feast! Yeah, the orchestra absolutely loves her, and her down-home, elegant performances are a highlight of every JALC season.

DIANNE REEVES
VOCALIST

JAZZ.

From the moment I walked through Frederick P. Rose Hall's artists' entrance for the opening gala, it felt as if I had entered a family reunion. This was surely a new place I would be calling home.

Among my fondest memories from numerous appearances since was the Katrina Benefit, an event filled with an extraordinary assemblage of artists who were there to take care of the business at hand. Immediately following the fundraiser, something unforgettable unfolded. It was less a jam session than a musical gathering, which provided an emotional release for the New Orleans musicians present—a large contingent. Offstage, in the house, drummer Herlin Riley led a spiritual experience filled with music, dancing, and tears as he paid homage to the legacy of New Orleans. It was an outpouring thick with tradition that went on for some time, and everyone's spirits were lifted to the heavens. This kind of moment—and there have been many others—cannot happen just anywhere; this is the kind of thing that only happens at a sacred space . . . at a "home." Rich with a ceaseless musical spirit, Jazz at Lincoln Center is a home to jazz in so many ways, and I am thankful for its existence. Amen.

PURPOSE 143

AFTER WE OPENED THE HALL, WE WERE UNDER CONSTANT FINANCIAL pressure. When Lisa Schiff and I would scour the city for money, I would say, "We're like sharecroppers from Mississippi who have just inherited a mansion and now have to keep the lights on." It seemed like overnight we went from a budget of $12 million with a staff of fifty-three in 2002 to a budget of $30 million with a staff of 125 in 2005. Lisa said people she knew would leave the room as she entered so as not to discuss jazz and money. At one point she told me, "I didn't envision my sixties going this way, okay?" Still, we just weren't going to let this fail. When New Orleans was devastated by Hurricane Katrina in August of 2005, JALC was in no position to help. Every dollar we raised had to go to our unnerving bottom line. Fortunately, no one informed André Guess. At the time he was our vice president and producer of programming and concert operations. A man of profound ideas, he left us no choice.

ANDRÉ KIMO STONE GUESS
FORMER VICE PRESIDENT
AND PRODUCER
JAZZ AT LINCOLN CENTER

ON SATURDAY AUGUST 27, 2005, David Gibson (production), Susan John (touring), and I boarded a plane at Louis Armstrong International Airport in New Orleans to head back to New York City. We were winding up a multiday planning excursion for the Congo Square Festival with the Jazz at Lincoln Center Orchestra for the spring of 2006. There was a palpable sense of unease in the Crescent City that day as the gulf coast began to prepare for their unwelcomed guest—Ms. Katrina.

Upon returning home, I watched the death, devastation, and destruction in horror with the rest of the world. Like many, I felt powerless to help beyond prayer, but quickly realized that there were resources at my disposal that could not only help but could also promote healing. Jazz at Lincoln Center could do a concert to benefit the displaced cultural community in New Orleans, particularly jazz musicians. It seemed natural that we stand in service to the city and the continuum of musicians that gave birth to our art form.

The entire leadership and staff at JALC were on board. We began to assemble a team that could make the impossible possible, in less than two weeks. I called my friend and colleague Michael Cuscuna to see if he would assist in producing the concert. He not only agreed but also offered, on behalf of Blue Note Records, to produce a CD whose proceeds would go toward the benefit. John Goberman, executive producer of *Live from Lincoln Center*, agreed to produce the show for PBS. I knew that David Gibson, our director of production, would be able to coordinate all of the technical, production, and logistical aspects of the event.

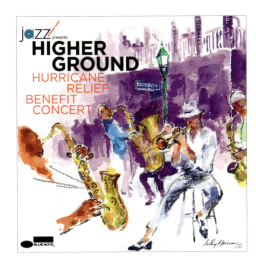

LEFT: JALC *Higher Ground* concert CD.

BELOW: *Higher Ground* second line, 2005.

OPPOSITE, TOP: Humanity Street, Hurricane Katrina, 2005.

OPPOSITE, BOTTOM: Baptist Drum, Hurricane Katrina, 2005.

Normally, a show that included Bill Cosby, Laurence Fishburne, James Taylor, Norah Jones, Paul Simon, Toni Morrison, Glenn Close, Shirley Caesar, Abbey Lincoln, and Herbie Hancock would have made me a nervous wreck. This, however, was one of the easiest concerts we ever produced. Many of the so-called stars who were used to being catered to went out of their way to tend to the needs of their fellow artists.

The sheer outpouring of unconditional love and empathy shown by a broad cross-section of the arts and entertainment community renewed my faith in humanity. The five-hour marathon went off without a hitch and culminated with a second line throughout Rose Theater. As we sang, shouted, and danced up and down the aisles, I couldn't help but think that we were symbolically giving a jazz funeral to the hundreds of people who were not afforded a proper burial. In the process, we were giving the living a much-needed reminder of the healing power of music. I remember dancing alongside then–Lieutenant Governor of Louisiana Mitch Landrieu in the second line and seeing and feeling the emotion pouring out of him. He, like many others that night, especially those from New Orleans, benefited in ways that money can't buy. But money can help! We raised over three million dollars that was distributed to New Orleans arts organizations, artists, and their families. This was by far the proudest moment of my tenure at Jazz at Lincoln Center.

TOP: *Higher Ground* second line, 2005.

TOP RIGHT: Toni Morrison, *Higher Ground*, 2005.

ABOVE: Robin Williams, *Higher Ground*, 2005.

RIGHT: James Taylor, *Higher Ground*, 2005.

RIGHT: Herlin Riley, *Higher Ground* second line, 2005.

BELOW: Mark O'Connor and Renée Fleming, 2005.

BELOW, CENTER: Don Vappie and Cassandra Wilson join the second line, *Higher Ground*, 2005.

BELOW, RIGHT: Ashley Schiff at the *Higher Ground* rehearsal, 2005.

BOTTOM: Dianne Reeves, *Higher Ground*, 2005.

PURPOSE 147

TOP: Aria Summers, two years old, shows us all how to second line.

TOP RIGHT: Laurence Fishburne, *Higher Ground*, 2005.

ABOVE: Ken Burns, *Higher Ground*, 2005.

RIGHT: Buckwheat Zydeco, accordian player, and Paul Simon, *Higher Ground*, 2005.

RIGHT: Aaron Neville at the *Higher Ground* benefit in 2005.

BELOW: *Higher Ground* audience, Frederick P. Rose Hall, 2005.

ABOVE, TOP: Wynton Marsalis, Vincent Gardner, and Ali Jackson dancing with Cuban ladies, Havana, Cuba, 2010.

ABOVE: A 2,000-year-old Roman amphitheater, Vienne, France.

AFTER A GALA HONORING THE GREAT TITO PUENTE IN November 2001, we all felt that his and the music of other great Afro-Latin composers would be better served by a band of specialists in that style. We asked Arturo O'Farrill if he would develop and lead an ensemble. Since 1995, he had a regular gig at Birdland leading The Afro-Cuban Jazz Orchestra that played much of the music of his father, Chico O'Farrill.

The Afro-Latin Jazz Orchestra of Jazz at Lincoln Center performed their first concert on October 25, 2002. They played in the tradition of Afro-Latin jazz, commissioned new compositions, and conducted education workshops. During their three-season tenure at JALC, they also toured fifty-six cities and created a beautiful original ballet, *Palladium Night*, in the Rose Theater in collaboration with Ballet Hispanico.

With the strain of inhabiting the new building and insufficient forward planning, we lacked the staff and organizational infrastructure to sustain two orchestras. If you ever want to know why consultants take so much time, and charge so much money, this scenario would provide a perfect answer. The art and spirit was right, but our ambition exceeded our assets. In 2007, Arturo and I agreed that the ALJO would continue as an independent entity. Shortly thereafter, they took up residence at Symphony Space and five years later they continue to serve communities everywhere under the umbrella of the Afro-Latin Jazz Alliance with a mission of preservation, innovation, education, and performance.

Performances galvanize people. When someone is touched by any aspect of a concert experience, the landscape of their life is changed. That's why the orchestra loves to see board members like Keith Reinhard, Stephen Daniel, and family and staff members at rehearsals and gigs. At a reception for the JLCO and the Berlin Philharmonic at the American Academy in Berlin, board member John Arnhold introduced the entire band from memory. All the cats talked about it, the personal touch that makes things shine. Jimmy Hamilton played with the great Duke Ellington Orchestra. He played in one of JALC's first orchestras and told us Duke used to say, "Get off the page and personalize your parts." That's what we want every JALC concert to be. And there have been many like that. This is a roll call of performances that stand out in our collective memories:

THAT FIRST DUKE ELLINGTON CONCERT, which misnamed a tribute in August of '**88**. **MR. JELLY LORD** of '**89**, when those men from New Orleans came up and created new fans of Jelly Roll's music with some of the most homespun transcriptions ever. **SOLO MONK** in July of '**91** with **TODD WILLIAMS** playing the tenor saxophone and ham boning on legs and chest. **BETTY CARTER**'s classic in March of '**92**, **THE MUSIC NEVER STOPS,** which was followed up by **CELIA CRUZ**'s December fiesta classic, **CELEBRATION CON CELIA,** which had people dancing in the aisles of Alice Tully Hall. **THE FIRST JAZZ FOR YOUNG PEOPLE** in '**92** with those handmade posters no one in the audience could read. The **TONY BENNETT** concert in January of '**94** that continued into the night. **KANSAS SWING AND SHOUT** right after it in August, when **JAY MCSHANN** and **CLAUDE "FIDDLER" WILLIAMS** came out east and showed us again what that Midwestern stomp was all about. **BLOOD ON THE FIELDS** of '**94** with a band of youngsters, many of whom I had taught in classes as kids. The really poorly played **SMALL BAND CONCERT OF LOUIS ARMSTRONG MUSIC** that caused **ED BRADLEY** to threaten to leave the board if we ever did that again. **THE CARNEGIE HALL JAZZ BAND** jumping on us in June of '**94** (even **FIDDLER WILLIAMS** couldn't bail us out). **DUKE IN HOLLYWOOD** of '**96** with **MADELINE PEYROUX**, evoking the ghost of Billie Holiday in the third movement of "Symphony in Black." What about **MARCUS ROBERTS**'s *EVOLUTION OF BLUES AND SWING IN 3 PARTS* in the elegantly lit Kaplan Penthouse throughout the '**96**–'**97** season? Our posthumous concert for **GERRY MULLIGAN** in '**96** that featured a band brought up from New Orleans, at his request, to celebrate his life. And the Masters come to New York from Cuba including **NICO ROJAS**, **CHUCHO VALDÉS**, **FRANK EMILIO**, **CACHAÍTO**, and **CHANGUITO** in January of '**98** to set Alice Tully Hall agroove. The super-soulful **HAROLD ASHBY** reading a letter he received from **BEN WEBSTER** upon joining Ellington on the Ellington Alumni panel on January 14, **1999**. **JOHN LEWIS** getting the JLCO to play softly and in balance in '**99**'s *JUMP FOR JOY*. (I did not play on this concert. After the performance, I asked Wess, "How did he do it?" He replied, "He just looked at us and we knew we were bullshitting, and we stopped.")

WYCLIFFE GORDON's southern score in September of **2000** for **OSCAR MICHEAUX**'s silent film, *Body and Soul*. A collaboration with the Film Society of Lincoln Center provided many memorable themes, and we teased **RODNEY WHITAKER** that he looked like the reverend in the film. **DIANNE REEVES**'s stellar Valentine's Day concert in **2001**, followed by another **MARCUS ROBERTS** solo piano classic a couple of months later in Avery Fisher. We threw **DANCE PARTIES** at the Manhattan Center all throughout **2000** and **2001**, and inaugurated **SINGERS OVER MANHATTAN** with **VANESSA RUBIN** and **KEVIN MAHOGANY**. **ABBEY LINCOLN** graced our stages with an Anthology of Her Compositions and Poems in March of '**02** and left folks gasping for more. **CHANO DOMINGUEZ** joined us in '**03** to show us that a collaboration could also fulfill the objectives of jazz and launched a relationship between the **JLCO** and his **FLAMENCO JAZZ ENSEMBLE** that has intensified over time.

ORNETTE COLEMAN came to hear our arrangements of his music on February 19, **2004**, and was surprised by the flexibility of the big band. **DAVE BRUBECK'S OCTET** on March 22 of that same year, which featured **BOBBY MILITELLO**, who electrified the audience in Avery Fisher Hall with clarity and purpose. In September of '**05**, we served barbecue in the lobby and swung to **KANSAS CITY SWING** in the Rose and rocked to **BOBBY WATSON WITH KANSAS CITY BOOGIE WOOGIE** in the Allen Room. **CECIL TAYLOR** and **JOHN ZORN** played their brand of improvised music. **TED NASH**'s masterful collaboration with the **MUSEUM OF MODERN ART** in '**07**, "Portrait in Seven Shades," that inspired the talents of the ten arrangers in the **JLCO**. **GIL EVANS**'s family came out and enjoyed Sketches of Gil Evans (we got to play with a bassoon, always an honor), while in '**08**, **MONTY ALEXANDER** told us about the Lords of the West Indies and everybody was ready to go down there.

In '**09** we turned our arrangers loose on **NURSERY SONG SWING**, which everybody thought was a dumb idea at first, but after they heard it changed their minds or at least said they did. **ORNETTE COLEMAN** opened the '**09** season to great fanfare. It was packed to the rafters and was filled with the type of shamanistic magic only he can conjure. We celebrated the **MARY LOU WILLIAMS CENTENNIAL**, and playing her music made us understand once again how much music she could write and play. **GERI ALLEN** lifted us with sophisticated harmonic explorations, rhythmic drive, and sympathetic comping. In '**10 MARIO ADNET** brought us the music of the **BRAZILIAN DUKE ELLINGTON**, **MOACIR SANTOS**, and we realized how much more of his music we need to hear. **CHICK COREA** enlightened our orchestra with his encyclopedic knowledge and total dedication. In '**11**, our arrangers went to work on his music and he responded with a contagious enthusiasm. **LEWIS NASH**, **KENNY BARRON**, **PETER WASHINGTON**, and **STEVE NELSON** played the music of the Modern Jazz Quartet to a fare-thee-well in the Allen Room in April of '**11**. In October, we celebrated my fiftieth birthday for what seemed like a month. But a lot of great artists performed at these concerts: **MARK O'CONNOR**, **BRANFORD MARSALIS**, **JARED GRIMES**, **YACUB ADDY AND ODADAA!**, **DAMIEN SNEED**, and **THE CHORALE LE CHATEAU**. And **CHRIS CRENSHAW** and **SHERMAN IRBY** wrote two original compositions that actually received standing ovations on opening night, May 17, **2012**, when usually all you hear with new music is crickets (I'm speaking from personal experience). Chris's piece was based on James Weldon Johnson's **GOD'S TROMBONES** and Sherman's was a ballet based on **DANTE'S INFERNO**. Both works were tour de forces and required tremendous concentration.

IT IS BY NO COINCIDENCE THAT THE PERSON WHO DREAMED about a jazz presence at Lincoln Center, Alina Bloomgarden, also worked in visitors services. This department is always the closest to the audience. In our Hall, the volunteers that work the visitors services desk are pure soul and dedication. Led by the evangelical and inspirational Rosemary Rutledge, they are knowledgeable and enthusiastic about how we deliver our mission. The volunteers always have engaging stories to tell.

ROSEMARY RUTLEDGE
DIRECTOR OF VISITORS SERVICES
JAZZ AT LINCOLN CENTER

DATE NIGHT AT JALC:

A young couple walked up to the fifth floor one spring evening looking for "the free jazz concert." That evening there were Dizzy's sets, but nothing that fit the description of "free." I asked the man if he knew the concert location. He said he thought it was somewhere at Lincoln Center, but that he had already been there and they sent him to us. His date looked tired and frustrated, which didn't bode well for him. The two of us at the desk started scouring the Thursday jazz listings and the Lincoln Center concert schedule. Do you know who was playing? No. Do you remember anything about the venue? No. Big band or small group? He didn't know. It was looking unlikely that we would be able to find what he was looking for and, furthermore, his date was becoming increasingly disenchanted with each minute. We continued to search for "free jazz" events, but could see that his plan for the evening had been foiled and he needed a new strategy. I told him I couldn't seem to find anything under free concerts for the evening, and usually we're the first to know what's happening jazzwise in the neighborhood. That said, Dizzy's had a great late set in an hour and entry was $5 a head if they still wanted to catch some music. We asked if they would like to take a peek into the Allen Room while they reconsidered their plans. His date still looked unenthused, but agreed. That night the Allen Room was dark, so as we walked in, all you could focus on was the view of Columbus Circle and the city lights across the park. The woman's eyes lit up at the sight of the window and she walked right up to the glass, nose almost touching it. For a while, the three of us just stood there in silence, faces peering through the glass watching taxis round the circle. We went wordless for a few more minutes until the man noted out loud, "No one ever looks up in New York." I smiled, "I know, they have no idea what they are missing." They laughed and thanked me for the tour. "Where to next?" I asked. "To Dizzy's, I think." She smiled, took his hand, and they walked out toward the club.

ABOVE: Bebo Valdés and the Afro-Latin Jazz Orchestra, Frederick P. Rose Hall, 2006.

LEFT: Trumpet section of the Afro-Latin Jazz Orchestra, Frederick P. Rose Hall, 2006.

OPPOSITE: Todo Tango and the Afro-Latin Jazz Orchestra, Frederick P. Rose Hall, 2006.

COMMUNICATIONS

PREVIOUS PAGE: Gala dinner setting in the Allen Room.

TOP: Wynton Marsalis, Ali Jackson, drummer, and Willie Nelson in 2009.

TOP, RIGHT: Bob Dylan with JLCO at the 2004 Spring Gala.

ABOVE: B.B. King and Eric Clapton with JLCO at the 2003 Spring Gala.

RIGHT: Aretha Franklin performing at the 2009 Spring Gala.

FAR RIGHT: Paul Simon and Mark Stewart, Simon's musical director, performing at the 2012 Spring Gala.

FOR OUR 2002 FALL GALA, AUGUST WILSON GIFTED US WITH a Harlem street scene. This excerpt perfectly captures the spirit of the many artists who have contributed their time and efforts to our cause.

SADIE *comes up the street singing.*

The song is a dirge, a lament, a beggar's plea, a healing song. It is all of these things and comes from deep inside her, something old, a wound that has now become an indelible mark. The song is the only thing she has and, in a moment of great selflessness, she gives that to the world, pushing it out past her lips to compete with the other sounds of the street. It is in the giving of this song that she finds a wholeness, a balance, a value to her person.

WHAT MAKES ERIC CLAPTON DONATE a week of his time to a charity, rehearse and play concerts, learn new arrangements, and front an unfamiliar band, in public? Paul Simon underwrote a week of rehearsals to play three free concerts. Ruth Brown, John Legend, Natalie Merchant, John Mayer, and Stevie Wonder are just a few that have helped support JALC over the years. We will never forget Tony Bennett stepping up for us in the early years, making himself available at no charge, and at the very last minute. Tony once called me just to say, "Thank you for stressing the importance of Louis Armstrong. People forget as the time passes, but we all come from him. Good-bye."

Artists of all genres, from Jessye Norman to Eddie Palmieri to Woody Allen and Bob Dylan to Aretha Franklin and Jimmy Buffet, have graced our stages and rehearsal halls to help keep us solvent. There are so many experiences. For example, Ray Charles, who was not a man given to gratuitous displays of emotion, loved Willie Nelson. Just watching it was instructional. Bob Dylan wrote a message to the band the day after his performance that in essence said, "It was a pleasure doing those old tunes in a new way. We should do it again sometime."

I was never enthusiastic about doing galas that didn't feature jazz. But I learned something valuable from performing with each person, regardless of idiom, who donated their time and energy. Diana Ross was the first person who made me understand that in performance there is something deeper and more primal than even the art itself: charisma. I was reticent to approach her and remained quietly in the trumpet section as she entered the room to rehearse. The rehearsal was tense. Later, she asked me why I didn't welcome her properly to the room (like any good host should). It was actually sweet and something my mama would have said. That made me realize that being a person should always come before anything else, and fame is only a mask. In the concert, she was electric.

Musicians love to listen to each other and to sound good together. It's mystical. You're in a room talking, then in the next moment, a skill can put you all in another universe of feeling. Music. Recordings don't do justice to the intimacy of playing. To feel Bill Cosby's timing or the drive of Eric Clapton's rhythm playing, the superslow phrasing of Ray Charles or the unpredictable improvisations of Willie Nelson made us all better, more complete musicians. Experiencing their largesse,

LEFT: Harry Connick Jr. performing with the JLCO at the 1999 Fall Gala.

OPPOSITE: Ashley Schiff, chair of the Fundraising Gala Committee, thanking the sponsors at the 2006 Spring Gala.

singularity of purpose, and dedication to excellence when rehearsing and performing made us all deeper, more engaged people, and it enriched our institution. "Thank you" is almost an insult.

The Fall Gala was always our signature event. It provided our board the opportunity to tell the whole community how much they loved and supported the organization. And they did it with style. Everyone was dressed to the nines, and the spaces overflowed with the feeling of prom-night pomp that always comes with tuxes and gowns, corsages and shiny shoes. We were able to give awards and publicly say positive things about people we loved. The band was on point for the concert, though we would sometimes lose focus during the after-concert dance, where spirits were lifted and imbibed.

The script was always a problem. Our annual host was the sartorially resplendent journalist Ed Bradley. He was a script taskmaster. Ed would tell you if he didn't like a concert, too! But he always hated this script. Two minutes before he's about to go on the Avery Fisher Hall stage in front of a packed house, he would still be editing his script. Calling me over, he'd say, "This script is a mess. Who wrote this shit? We're not in Kenner [Louisiana]. This is New York.

What *looks* good doesn't necessarily *sound* good." He would go on making corrections with some type of under-the-breath adjectives. Then, seconds before stage time, he'd say, "How you like these shoes?" As he walked out, he'd wink and say, "Have a great concert, man." Once, at the end of a spirited board meeting, Ed and David Stern put up a substantial sum of money, auction-style, to save our radio show for another year. Now we give the Ed Bradley Award annually at the gala, but we sure do miss him.

In a 1992 brochure we wrote, "A crucial part of our vision involves utilizing jazz to inspire a variety of oft-neglected conversations: among groups and voices separated by geography, economic status, or race, among the various disciplines of the arts, and among generations. When we distance ourselves from each other, we distance ourselves from the profundity of our democratic heritage." Ashley Schiff was a high school student when those words were written. What she was to accomplish in support of our mission was unprecedented and nothing less than astounding. Though by far our youngest board member, she showed us what was possible in the largely segregated cultural community of New York City.

WHEN I HEARD WYNTON MARSALIS

ASHLEY SCHIFF
CHAIR OF FUNDRAISING
GALA COMMITTEE
JAZZ AT LINCOLN CENTER

When I heard Wynton Marsalis with the Lincoln Center Jazz Orchestra (as it was then called) in Buenos Aires in November of 1998 at the Teatro Gran Rex, I was twenty-four and it made a huge impression on me. What Wynton preached about great music transcending the generation gap and bringing people of all backgrounds together seemed so true in Argentina, especially in their enthusiastically received concert, but much less so back at home in the staid, imposing halls of Lincoln Center.

The experience of that time on the road gave me the desire to create a different type of concert back home, a collaborative performance that would inspire new people to become as excited as I was about jazz.

In the spring of 2001, I asked artist Jennifer Bartlett to host a cocktail party to begin building buzz around a benefit to attract a younger, broader cross-section of New Yorkers than normally supported most Lincoln Center events.

I tried to invite all the brightest and most energetic young professionals I knew at the time to join the Jazz Associates Committee. This committee would host the concert. Fortunately, we were able to get the Apollo Theater for a night, free of charge. So, we had the perfect location. But the work was only beginning. My friend Darren Walker walked me door to door in Harlem to get the community energized, and we were on our way to something new.

Musically, we focused on Wynton's septet—the group of mostly New Orleans musicians who played with him before the formation of the orchestra. It included Herlin Riley, Reginald Veal, Victor Goines, Wycliffe Gordon, Wessell "Warmdaddy" Anderson, and the piano player most appropriate at the time. They were the "best of the best," which meant they could learn any arrangement, in any style, in a very short time.

This was to be JALC's spring benefit. There was not huge support for this second benefit, and expectations were set accordingly—the hope was that we could raise $400,000, and, after September 11, 2001, many people thought I should cancel the idea of a benefit entirely.

There were, of course, many trials and tribulations in presenting this concert off Lincoln Center's campus. Just the negotiations with PS 154 Harriet Tubman, the school behind the Apollo, to tent their playground for the postconcert dinner would take several chapters to discuss. But miraculously, we did it. With a lineup of Whoopi Goldberg hosting, and Sir Roland Hanna, Vanessa Williams, Savion Glover, and Stevie Wonder, we raised $950,000 that first year. The show told the story of jazz in Harlem, and we even did a jazz version of Stevie's classic, "Living for the City." The next year, the *New York Times* style section proclaimed our benefit one of the only truly integrated functions in New York.

Since that year, we have hosted Jimmy Buffett, Ray Charles, Tracy Chapman, Eric Clapton, Joe Cocker, Lou Donaldson, Robert Downey Jr., Bob Dylan, Roland Hanna, Al Jarreau, Tom Jones, Wynonna Judd, B.B. King, Lenny Kravitz, John Legend, Lyle Lovett, Branford Marsalis, John Mayer, Audra McDonald, Natalie Merchant, Willie Nelson, Carrie Smith, Kevin Spacey, James Taylor, Derek Trucks, and Susan Tedeschi, with hosts such as Chevy Chase, Bernie Mac, Cedric the Entertainer, Laurence Fishburne, and Don Cheadle. And those concerts have led into full-scale, incredibly successful collaborations with Willie Nelson, Eric Clapton, and Paul Simon.

There have been many funny stories in those years as well as crippling moments when we weren't sure how things would turn out. But all of the musicians we have worked with have been in awe of how they were treated by JALC, and how seriously we took their music. Besides their obvious generosity, these artists have been wonderful personally and always leave saying they would like to work with us again. Most of all, many come in intimidated to play with jazz musicians they hold in such high esteem, but leave feeling embraced and welcomed.

The warmth and jubilation at these events made New York seem like a small community coming together and, as Whoopi Goldberg said the first year, made us feel like we were all just at one great big rent party. And what is better than that?

LEFT: Fantasia performing with the JLCO at the 2007 Fall Gala.

BELOW, LEFT: The Woody Allen Band performing at the 2002 Fall Gala.

BELOW, CENTER: Saxophonists Joe Lovano and Branford Marsalis at the 2004 Fall Gala.

BELOW: Diana Ross with JLCO at the 2003 Fall Gala.

JALC HONOREES

Jazz at Lincoln Center is proud to honor those individuals who have made an enormous impact on jazz artistically, culturally, and institutionally. It offers three awards, for Artistic Excellence, Lifetime Achievement, and Leadership. The Leadership Award was renamed the Ed Bradley Award in 2007 to celebrate our friend and board member Ed Bradley, who served on the JALC board from 1992 until his untimely death in 2007. The following is a list of honorees:

NOVEMBER 18, 1996
Lionel Hampton: Artistic Excellence
George Weissman: Leadership

NOVEMBER 10, 1997
Oscar Peterson: Artistic Excellence
Ahmet Ertegun: Leadership

NOVEMBER 2, 1998
Benny Carter: Artistic Excellence
June Noble Larkin: Leadership

NOVEMBER 1, 1999
John Lewis: Artistic Excellence
Irene Diamond: Leadership
Norman Granz: Lifetime Achievement

NOVEMBER 13, 2000
Illinois Jacquet: Artistic Excellence
Jack and Susan Rudin: Leadership
Nathan Leventhal: Founders

NOVEMBER 12, 2001
Chico O'Farrill: Artistic Excellence
Gordon J. Davis: Leadership
George Wein: Lifetime Achievement

NOVEMBER 11, 2002
Max Roach: Artistic Excellence
Village Vanguard accepted by Lorraine Gordon: Leadership

NOVEMBER 17, 2003
Shirley Horn: Artistic Excellence
Phoebe Jacobs: Leadership

OCTOBER 20, 2004
No awards given

NOVEMBER 14, 2005
Hughlyn F. Fierce: Leadership

NOVEMBER 13, 2006
No awards given

NOVEMBER 2, 2007
Ed Bradley: posthumously awarded the Ed Bradley Award

NOVEMBER 10, 2008
Ken Burns: Ed Bradley Award

NOVEMBER 17, 2009
Albert Murray: Ed Bradley Award

MAY 17, 2010
No awards given

APRIL 7, 2011
Dr. Billy Taylor: Ed Bradley Award

APRIL 18, 2012
Lisa Schiff: Ed Bradley Award

ABOVE, TOP: Liza Minnelli performing with the JLCO at the 2004 Fall Gala.
ABOVE: Guitarist Derek Trucks performing with the JLCO at the 2007 Spring Gala.

INTEGRITY

MARCUS ROBERTS HAS GRACED OUR STAGES 148 TIMES. He performed on our second concert, The Music of Thelonious Monk, August 4, 1987. We call him "the genius of the modern piano," and he is unwavering in his pursuit of the deepest, most meaningful notes. One note, and you know he means what he is saying.

MARCUS ROBERTS
PIANIST, ASSISTANT PROFESSOR OF JAZZ STUDIES
FLORIDA STATE UNIVERSITY

INTEGRITY GUARANTEES

that the important achievements and contributions of one generation will still be available for generations to come. It is a mandate that protects our highest ideals and provides examples for us to follow. I believe that the value of one's integrity grows over time, because as time goes by, life affords us with more and more opportunities to live either in accordance with our own values or to violate those principles. For a musician, integrity is earned by continuing to work toward our artistic goals, despite the obstacles and adversities that may be placed in our path. Without integrity, very little is sacred or really safe. It cannot be taken away, but it can be cast aside. It's up to us.

My goals as an artist have always been the same: to present a modern view of jazz piano, grounded in creating a dialogue with the many great pianist/composers throughout history; to gain inspiration and knowledge from classical composers; to teach and mentor students; and to develop a compositional and band sound and style that are individual and recognizable by musicians and the public. Over the years, I have been blessed to be able to pursue those goals in solo piano, trio, nonet, big band, and orchestral settings at Jazz at Lincoln Center. The most essential quality of our music and of this institution is that we believe in the inclusion, not exclusion, of all cultural groups in what we do. We want everyone to dig the music and participate in it, and we have such a deep love and passion for jazz music that nothing will stop us from ensuring that our art form will flourish for generations to come.

PREVIOUS PAGE: JLCO encore in 2011.
OPPOSITE: Pianist Marcus Roberts.

CHRISTA TETER, TWENTY-SIX AT THE TIME SHE STARTED in 1996, was a production coordinator until 2004. She handled the music and musicians with uncommon grace and maturity.

CHRISTA TETER
FORMER PRODUCTION MANAGER
JAZZ AT LINCOLN CENTER

BAGELS, FRESH COFFEE, WATER, ONE TUNED PIANO, a drum kit, a

bass stool, twenty music stands, sharpened pencils, music, and musicians. It was another weekend morning at Carroll Music Studios, on Forty-First Street, and my job was to scurry around the studio to assemble the above requirements for a successful rehearsal. Knowing that Sunday mornings are tough for a jazz musician in New York City, I grabbed my bag of quarters and made reminder phone calls to the usual suspects' homes to ensure that they would be on time for *these* rehearsals. Production department meetings months before were laden with concerns about artist punctuality; the four days of rehearsals in April of 1998 would be different because John Lewis would be conducting the LCJO. So I knew the importance of timeliness for that week. Whenever Mr. Lewis attended meetings regarding the upcoming concerts, I took notice of Wynton's and Rob's enthusiasm and unwavering respect for him.

The former leader of the Modern Jazz Quartet was seventy-seven years old in 1998—he arrived fifteen minutes early at Carroll Music Studios wearing a tweed blazer, tie, khakis, briefcase, and a genuine smile. This was my first year as a production coordinator, so I had scrutinized his contract looking for the unusual requests from some artists, such as a white stretch limousine, guava juice, and sushi, but there were none; when I asked Mr. Lewis what he needed, he simply requested water and coffee. He was a true gentleman and professional, faithful to his work; he was not needy or pretentious, but he had high expectations of the artists and staff. I kept a close eye on the clock and waited impatiently for the band members to arrive. Heart pounding, I ran downstairs and out the door to look for the guys, as if my scanning and pacing on Forty-First Street would make them suddenly appear. "C'mon Wycliffe, Westray, please don't be late," I thought. To my good fortune, everyone arrived on time. The guys clearly held him in the highest esteem; they greeted him with polite handshakes and he reciprocated with smiles and used their first names that he had committed to memory. Like the eager feeling you get when you begin a new class with a professor you know will teach you a lot, the climate in the rehearsal studio that spring morning was one of

ABOVE: John Lewis conducting.

OPPOSITE: Christa Teter, former production manager.

determination, creativity, and enthusiasm. As a non-musician who observed these rehearsals from an objective viewpoint, I learned about inclusion, respect, kinship, and how all of the parts make up the whole. There was an overall positive, hopeful feeling between the artists and JALC staff that week. I felt proud and excited to be a part of this small organization that was determined to celebrate and teach jazz music to the world.

Mr. Lewis was a perfectionist and would gingerly inform the artists when something didn't sound right; he invested the necessary time to make this a fantastic show. Respecting Mr. Lewis and his decisions, the guys carefully marked up their music with the sharpened pencils. I learned how respect is contagious, and how when people respect each other, they work better together; when they work well together, they sound great; and when they sound great, they make everyone feel good.

That week in April 1998 culminated with me standing in a dark backstage, watching Mr. Lewis accept loud and extensive applause, and then receiving a warm hug, giant smile, and thank-you from a tired, but clearly satisfied, seventy-seven-year-old jazz icon. That moment stays in my heart, and I reflect on that memory often with gratitude. It was not just another weekend.

ALAN COHN, JOHN ARNHOLD, AND HUGH FIERCE watch over our finances like hawks. Hugh says, "Nothing has more integrity than numbers."

HUGHLYN FIERCE
FORMER PRESIDENT AND CEO, JAZZ AT LINCOLN CENTER

LOUD AND ALL DAY LONG,
Birdell's Record Shop on Fulton Street in Bed-Stuy played Charlie Parker and Dizzy Gillespie's *Ko-Ko*. It was 1947. I was twelve years old and loved it because Mama and my dad didn't.

They neither liked nor understood bebop or bop. Tell the truth, neither did I then. But because they were parents, anything they didn't like, I loved.

They loved the Mills Brothers; I was into bop. They liked Sonny Til and The Orioles; I liked Miles Davis. Daddy listened to spiritual quartet singers on Sunday mornings. I lingered and listened to jazz emanating from The Kingston Lounge ten blocks from Birdell's when I walked past after school. I tried to get in one evening when Kenny Dorham was playing. I was sixteen and ordered a scotch and bourbon. These became my first cool drinks. "Out . . . get out of here right now . . . Not left now . . . right now," bellowed the bartender, quite ticked at my young boldness.

Returned several days later and wiser. This time I didn't order anything. Just sat in the corner quietly and listened to Kenny play his trumpet. Man, he was cool. A guy was so drunk at a table in front of the bandstand, he let drop a bottle. It splintered to the floor with a crisp, piercing glass sound right in the middle of Kenny's solo on "Una Más." Kenny rented on President Street, a block away from my house on Carroll Street. Of course, I waited for him that night after the gig to get his reaction to the damned disturbance. Didn't faze Kenny. "Bop and jazz needs to be in the halls where people listen to the music." I never forgot what he said.

I was cool and that meant I listened to jazz. Shhh, no sounds when Lennie Tristano is wailing at the Village Vanguard or the Modern Jazz Quartet is holding court at Birdland.

In 1955, "the coldest winter" was well under way in Korea. I joined the army to get Uncle Sam to pay for my college education. Negotiated deployment to France, not cold Korea. I had to be near the Paris Cool School run by Miles, Baker, Mulligan, Powell. Sure, I listened to Basie and even Ellington at the Mars Bar in Paris. Some evenings, Barbara Hutton was there paying for GI drinks and Joe Williams was singing after a gig. Joe looked very cool with a glass of booze in his left hand, singing, telling lies, and snapping his fingers with his right. We were cool. No Dixieland: No loud noise. We listened to Dexter, Sonny, Monk, Coltrane, Bill Evans.

After an MBA, thirty-two years of Chase Manhattan Bank, semi-retirement, and presidency and CEO of Jazz at Lincoln Center, I had a leisurely

dinner with Stanley Crouch and Wynton Marsalis at Cher Lewis's dinner party in the Village. Louis Armstrong came up in conversation. I said that I really didn't care for his white handkerchief, shaky trumpet, grinning teeth, and "Hello Dolly" jazz.

Those two put forks down in unison and challenged. "Have you ever listened to Louis play his music?" from Stanley. "Sure 'Hello Dolly.' That's not Pops's jazz," slammed the artistic director of Jazz at Lincoln Center. "You have to listen to Armstrong of the twenties and the fifties."

"I don't like Dixieland," I mumbled, thinking Armstrong doesn't know nor play bop.

"Unless you have really listened to Pops, you shouldn't talk about him." Case closed from Wynton. I'd forgotten he was a fellow red beans New Orleans patriot.

Homework, that next weekend, I devoured everything I could about Louis Armstrong, born August 4, 1901. I bought every CD I could find and reread portions from my bookshelf: Gunther Schuller's *Early Jazz* and his second book, *Swing Era*. I played *West End Blues* at least ten times before it dawned on me that nobody in 1927 played trumpet like Louis Armstrong. Jabbo Smith was good, but he couldn't touch Louis. Bix was smooth, but he would confess not being in Armstrong's league. Sure, Dixieland or Louisiana jazz was "hot," but not in my Bed-Stuy, Queens, even Harlem or Paris, until one evening in an elegant apartment high over Fifty-Seventh Street in the center of Manhattan on a cool, clear evening. The musicians played Ellington's "Mood Indigo." "Drop Me Off In Harlem." Yes. Damn. Cool was all that and all right that evening, until.

Couldn't believe my ears.

A few months after my education and change of heart, one director hosted a Jazz at Lincoln Center fundraiser. The musicians broke out "Saint James Infirmary," "Tom Cat Blues," and other Louisiana—Louis Armstrong's music. I was seated comfortably in a deeply cushioned nineteenth-century French chair with a vintage French red burgundy in my hand with no thought of rising. When the musicians stood up, led by Wynton playing his trumpet, I had to stand up against my will. They started playing and dancing around the room with their faces in the air or bodies in a deep bow with legs, thighs, and arms moving up and down doing the "second line." Apparently, when you go to a burial in New Orleans, band members play a slow, sad, dragging, moaning, melodic dirge of musical notes. On the way home from the cemetery, the musicians, family, and friends celebrate by dancing and playing a glad, high-stepping second line. In this gorgeous apartment, the band members were dancing around the room with white handkerchiefs over their heads sending their respects.

Quietly, I said to no one, "Not me. I am cool and prefer bop. If the boys from the block saw me doing this, I would be banned from bop and lose my cool license." But then I thought about Kenny's prophetic words; our splendid Jazz at Lincoln Center facility with its halls, education rooms, recording capability, and windows that send jazz out to the world; and the considerable funds to be raised that night. Well, I reached for my white handkerchief from my outer breast pocket and hopped in front of Victor Goines, saxophone player extraordinaire, as he was about to make the turn into another room.

ABOVE: Wynton Marsalis soloing in 2001's *Pops: The Ambassador of Swing* in Alice Tully Hall.

OPPOSITE, TOP: Hughlyn Fierce, former JALC president and CEO, giving a speech during the 2005 Fall Gala.

OPPOSITE, BOTTOM: Wess Anderson in the Rose Rehearsal Studio in 1994.

INTEGRITY 169

SINCE 1987, JAZZ AT LINCOLN CENTER HAS…

Featured over **850** musicians

Produced more than **1,128** original concerts in the New York City area

Produced **52** Jazz for Young People concerts

Produced more than **224** American Music Abroad and NEA Jazz in the Schools concerts

Produced **444** Jazz for Young People on Tour concerts

Produced over **40** tours featuring the Jazz at Lincoln Center Orchestra with Wynton Marsalis, the Afro-Latin Jazz Orchestra, and other ensembles, which have reached more than **424** cities in **37** countries on **6** continents

Produced tours for **46** ensembles, visiting **116** countries through *The Rhythm Road: American Music Abroad* program

Sent more than **120,000** copies of **88** previously unavailable scores to more than **3,500** schools through the Essentially Ellington High School Jazz Band program

Published over **152** music scores of original arrangements by artists such as Duke Ellington, Louis Armstrong, Count Basie, Fletcher Henderson, and **2** interactive jazz curriculums for grades 4 to 12

Created **5** educational Web resources available to **MILLIONS** worldwide

Held **HUNDREDS** of workshops, clinics, and professional development opportunities for students and teachers around the globe

Raised over **$3.5 MILLION** for Jazz at Lincoln Center's Higher Ground Hurricane Relief Fund

Raised more than **$370,000,000** for JALC

Held over **600** development events

Produced, with Murray Street Productions, more than **160** hours of the Peabody Award–winning *Jazz from Lincoln Center* radio program

ABOVE: Chris Crenshaw in Cuba.

RIGHT: Wess Anderson, alto saxophonist, Victor Goines, clarinetist, Wynton Marsalis, and Ronald Westley, trombonist, at Frederick P. Rose Hall in 2004.

JAZZ AT LINCOLN CENTER RECORDINGS

1992
Portraits by Ellington (Sony/Columbia)

1993
The Fire of the Fundamentals (Sony/Columbia)

1994
They Came to Swing (Sony/Columbia)

1997
Jump Start and Jazz (Sony/Columbia)

Blood on the Fields (Sony/Columbia)

1999
Live in Swing City (Sony/Columbia)

Big Train (Sony/Columbia)

Sweet Release & Ghost Story (Sony Classical)

2002
All Rise (Sony/Columbia)

2004
The Lincoln Center Jazz Orchestra for Brooks Brothers (Brooks Brothers)

2005
Cast of Cats (Brooks Brothers)

A Love Supreme (Palmetto Records)

Don't Be Afraid: The Music of Charles Mingus (Palmetto Records)

Higher Ground: Hurricane Relief Benefit Concert (Blue Note)

2007
Congo Square (self-produced)

2008
Two Men with the Blues with Willie Nelson and Wynton Marsalis (Blue Note)

2010
Portrait in Seven Shades (self-produced)

Vitoria Suite (Emarcy)

2011
Wynton Marsalis & Eric Clapton Play the Blues (Warner Brothers)

Here We Go Again: Celebrating the Genius of Ray Charles (Blue Note)

2012
WeBop: A Family Jazz Party (self-produced)

JALC COMMISSIONED OR PREMIERED COMPOSITIONS AND ARRANGEMENTS

Since its inception, Jazz at Lincoln Center has commissioned or premiered compositions and arrangements from numerous artists, including the following:

Yacub Addy
Toshiko Akiyoshi
Geri Allen
Tim Armacost
Pablo Aslan
Darin Atwater
Kurt Bacher
David Berger
Terence Blanchard
Walter Blanding
Darius Brubeck
Chris Byars
Benny Carter
Regina Carter
Joe Chambers
Bill Charlap
Billy Childs
Chris Crenshaw
Richard DeRosa
Chano Dominguez
Paquito D'Rivera
Andy Farber
Art Farmer
Frank Foster
Bob Franceschini
Bill Frisell
Vincent Gardner
Victor Goines
Benny Golson
Wycliffe Gordon
L.W. "Slide" Hampton
Roy Hargrove
Barry Harris
Jimmy Heath
Joe Henderson
Carlos Henriquez
Freddie Hubbard
Sherman Irby
Chuck Israels
Ali Jackson

Paul Jeffrey
Hank Jones
Laura Kahle
Jason Lindner
Joe Lovano
Wynton Marsalis
Christian McBride
Charles McPherson
Jason Moran
Michael Philip Mossman
Gerry Mulligan
Ted Nash
Zim Ngqawana
Arturo O'Farrill
Chico O'Farrill
Nicholas Payton
Danilo Perez
Dafnis Prieto
Marcus Printup
Eric Reed
Herlin Riley
Sam Rivers
Marcus Roberts
Wallace Roney
Maria Schneider
Stephen Scott
Hervé Sellin
Martin Sheller
Wayne Shorter
Martial Solal
Katsuhiko Tanaka
Papo Vazquez
Emil Viklicky
Erica von Kleist
Doug Wamble
Deborah Weisz
Randy Weston
Ron Westray
Rodney Whitaker
Eli Yamin

JALC GALA GUEST ARTISTS

Since 1996 when Jazz at Lincoln Center became a constituent, the fundraising galas have featured guest artists including:

FALL GALAS

1996
Ed Bradley, Natalie Cole, Savion Glover, Ruth Brown

1997
Ed Bradley, Tommy Flanagan, Stefon Harris, Joe Henderson, Conrad Herwig, Dave Holland, Pete La Roca Sims, Chaka Khan, John Scofield

1998
Ann Hampton Callaway, Diana Krall, Bobby Short

1999
Milt Grayson, Roberta Gumbel, Bobby McFerrin, Joya Sherrill

2000
André De Shields, Dr. John, Jessye Norman, Warren Vaché

2001
Jose Madera, Tito Puente Orchestra, Johnny Rodriguez

2002
Woody Allen, Denyce Graves, Patti LuPone, Paul Simon, August Wilson

2003
Dee Dee Bridgewater, Anne Drummond, Roberta Flack, Shirley Horn, Dame Cleo Laine, Marian McPartland, Jennifer Sanon, Diana Ross, Erica von Kleist

2004
Patti Austin, Michel Camilo, Eldar Djangirov, Marcus Gilmore, Roy Haynes, Joe Lovano, Branford Marsalis, Liza Minnelli, Brian Strokes Mitchell, Eric Reed, Dianne Reeves

2005
The Alvin Ailey American Dance Theater, Kim Burrell, Hank Jones, Diana Krall, The Kronos Quartet, Joe Lovano, Herlin Riley, Marcus Roberts

2006
The American Composers Orchestra, Michael Feinstein, Kitty Carlisle Hart, Angela Lansbury, Marcus Roberts, Patti Austin

2007
Paul Anka, Fantasia, Eartha Kitt

2008
George Benson, Orchestra of St. Luke's

2009
Michael Feinstein, Diahann Carroll

SPRING GALAS

2002
Whoopi Goldberg, Savion Glover, Sir Roland Hanna, Vanessa Williams, Stevie Wonder

2003
Laurence Fishburne, Ray Charles, Eric Clapton, Lou Donaldson, B.B. King, Audra McDonald, Willie Nelson, Carrie Smith

2004
Cedric the Entertainer, Bob Dylan, Al Jarreau, Branford Marsalis, Reneé Olstead, James Taylor

2005
Don Cheadle, Robert Downey Jr., Tom Jones, Wynonna Judd, Lyle Lovett, The Blind Boys of Alabama

2006
Bernie Mac, Tracy Chapman, Joe Cocker, John Legend, John Mayer, Natalie Merchant

2007
Jimmy Buffett, Derek Trucks, Kevin Spacey, Lenny Kravitz, Barbara Cook, Chevy Chase, Susan Tedeschi

2008
Patti Austin, James Ingram

2009
Aretha Franklin

ANNUAL GALAS

2010
Gladys Knight

2011
Eric Clapton

2012
Paul Simon

IDENTITY

MARY FIANCE WAS TWENTY-TWO WHEN SHE JOINED JAZZ at Lincoln Center in 1992. Nobody's been with us longer. She is our institutional memory and has been the unofficial custodian of our legacy. This book would not be possible without her.

MARY FIANCE
DIRECTOR OF PUBLIC RELATIONS
JAZZ AT LINCOLN CENTER

PREVIOUS SPREAD: Vincent Gardner teaching students at a music school in Havana, Cuba, in 2010.

ABOVE: Herlin Riley adding his personal shorthand to an underwritten part in 2005.

OPPOSITE: Sir Roland Hanna cutting those dots in 1991.

WORKING AS A P.R. INTERN

in the summer of 1989—an epiphany, listening to Wynton and Dr. Michael White, Sweet Papa Don Vappie, and more greats perform and tell stories about the music. I wanted to wrap myself in it, and communicate the joy and the nourishment in this music to as many people as possible. It's never stopped; I've had the honor of spending my adult life being raised by jazz.

In January 1991, we reawakened America's consciousness about jazz and began to change our culture. It was a new mission. We were moving from a series of summer concerts to year-round programming, and the news made the front page of the *New York Times*.

It was taking shape. The rave reviews of Classical Jazz turned into some criticism about jazz not needing a canon. But the caravan moved on and it's never stopped. Frank Rich gave high praise in his *New York Times Magazine* cover story on Wynton. There was a photo shoot by Arthur Elgort for *Vogue* magazine and the orchestra's first tour. Many years later, Annie Leibovitz came to shoot fashion with the JLCO at rehearsal. She asked to come back and shoot the band without the models and jumbo fans because she just loved them and the music.

An artistic drive to collaborate with the New York City Ballet and all the constituents led to coverage beyond the music press. We were being talked about and written about in social, film, dance, classical, and business media, and expanding jazz into more and more conversations.

We collaborated with almost every organization on the campus, foreshadowing the press conference for constituency July 1, 1996. On the plaza of Lincoln Center the agreements were signed, and by order of Mayor Giuliani, July 1, 1996, was proclaimed "Jazz at Lincoln Center Day" in New York City.

Nelson Rockefeller's dream of bringing arts and audiences together by creating an integrated performing arts center was becoming a reality. Fifty years ago when Lincoln Center broke ground, someone held a sign proclaiming, "We want Jazz at Lincoln Center." It finally came true. With more and more education events, publications, and the first competition

IDENTITY

for big bands featuring Duke Ellington's original arrangements and compositions, and an increasing number of arts institutions seeking to program their own jazz concerts, the needle was moving forward in America. We could feel it.

Although I sat through thousands of car rides bringing musicians from interview to interview, dealt with millions of phone interviews and photo shoots, it never got old or tiring, only more inspiring. I can never forget Roy Haynes telling me he never thought he'd see this in his lifetime. I cried on our way to that radio interview just from the sheer joy of seeing this happen for him. And Benny Carter reminiscing and walking around Lincoln Center with me. He had grown up just behind the campus and said, "This is where my house used to stand." Mr. Carter wrote "Echoes of San Juan Hill" in 1996 for the JLCO. I remember roaming around Newark on the way to WBGO, our partner radio station for so many years, with James Moody showing me where he used to play as a boy. I also can't forget the interviews with Illinois Jacquet in his superbright red jacket. It was so much fun.

Backstage on tour with the JLCO, the ex-Ellington bassist Jimmy Woode told me, "These are not musicians. They are magicians." Audiences in Russia stood and clapped and danced as if we were at a rock concert. There was a look of joy on the faces of the Russian National Orchestra as they sat surrounding the band in collaboration on the stage, hearing them play for the first time. Small Russian student bands met us at airports and train stations to honor the band and play jazz for them. The feeling was spreading throughout the world at the speed of sound.

Touring was always exciting, and not just because of the music. From the hard work of managing logistics for flights and ground travel for the band and the equipment, to the creation of the itinerary books, to cases of music being left on the tarmac, to holding airplane doors open with my feet until Norris Turney or Milt Grayson got on the plane. These musicians didn't just play, they did interviews and press conferences and receptions and lessons backstage until the last student got to say hello or got an autograph. They were all there, always. They did anything we needed them to do to be of service to the music.

While backstage during one of those early concerts with Joe Henderson and Freddie Hubbard, Bill Cosby showed up. He wanted me to show him where the phone was. After many staircases and a full circle back to where we started, I admitted I was lost, and our friendship began. Later, at the Jazz à Vienne festival in France, we plotted a surprise for the orchestra as he came out midshow pretending to be the roadie. There was about five minutes of laughter from the audience and the band.

I remember the joy of Betty Carter's full concert of song at the Lehman Center for the Arts in the Bronx and at Alice Tully Hall, and the words of Stanley Crouch after seeing *Blood on the Fields:* "Something incredibly special just happened in there." No matter what section, whether it was a front-page story or not, constant coverage continued to grow as we expanded our concert offerings, education programs, and Peabody Award–winning radio shows.

ABOVE: The importance of written music. JLCO performing at Rose Hall in 2009.

OPPOSITE: Wynton Marsalis composing in 2002.

RIGHT: Wess "Warmdaddy" Anderson in 1996 handling a difficult part in *Sweet Release*, a collaboration with Alvin Ailey American Dance Theater.

FAR RIGHT: Collaboration between Wynton Marsalis and Eric Clapton in 2011.

RIGHT, BOTTOM: Dan Nimmer in Havana with a Cuban piano student in 2010.

ABOVE, TOP: Jon Faddis, trumpeter, Wynton Marsalis, and John Lewis, pianist, during a 1997 rehearsal.

ABOVE: Vincent Gardner, trombonist, and Jerry Dodgion, saxophonist, seeing and hearing the music.

ABOVE, RIGHT: Wycliffe Gordon corrects his score.

RIGHT: Bobby Watson conducts the JLCO in a 2002 celebration of Art Blakey's Jazz Messengers.

ABOVE: Empire State Building jam session in 2006 with Vincent Gardner on the trombone.

RIGHT: Silhouette of Dan Nimmer immersed in an involved piano part.

RIGHT, BOTTOM: Marcus Printup and Ted Nash discuss their arrangements of Chick Corea's composition.

When the Smithsonian decided to shine a light on the music by declaring April Jazz Appreciation Month, we turned the Empire State Building blue and handed out beads and umbrellas as members of the JLCO performed a second line parade on the observation deck. We didn't know there would be a snowstorm in April! That made the cover of the *New York Sun*. We embraced Fleet Week in New York City, as Wynton and Harry Smith from CBS's *The Early Show* handed out tickets to the navy cadets and the marines so they could check out some real jazz during their week in town.

There were the thousands of stories for the construction and opening of the new building, and suddenly jazz was all over the architecture and real estate section. Wynton encouraged an air, land, and sea approach, and we followed with the cover of airline magazines that board members like Diane Coffey would pull out at a meeting and say, "Did you see this, right in everyone's seat pocket on the airplane!"

During the *Vanity Fair* photo shoot, the August moon was going fast across the sky and was visible through the Allen Room window. We all just stood still to look. That was the iconic view that would physically put us in the skyline and the landscape of New York City.

There were times I was so in awe of the artists and their artistry and reputation that I was intimidated. I remember taking Todd Barkan and Vincent Bly with me to Abbey Lincoln's house for a *New York Times* photo shoot. She could not have been more welcoming and gracious. I also remember Wynton on the phone with Fletcher Roberts at the *New York Times* describing Abbey's upcoming concerts. It was so inspiring; the *Times* ran two separate stories on her for those shows.

From continent to continent, there were friendly and unfriendly articles written. But we were there. From cover stories in small towns to seven-person production crews, from *60 Minutes* with Morley Safer, we were there, showing the world the power of jazz.

We are there.

JALC 25-YEAR TIMELINE

1987

The Jazz Committee of the Board of Directors of Lincoln Center for the Performing Arts, led by Gordon J. Davis, Board Chairman George Weissman, and President Nathan Leventhal, support Alina Bloomgarden's production of the first Classical Jazz Series with Artistic Director Wynton Marsalis, Artistic Consultant Stanley Crouch, and Historian Albert Murray.

1988

Jazz at Lincoln Center Orchestra forms with members of the Duke Ellington Orchestra and members of the Wynton Marsalis Septet. David Berger is conductor.

The Jazz at Lincoln Center Orchestra performs Ellington masterpieces that had not been performed for more than a quarter century: *Such Sweet Thunder*, *Suite Thursday*, and *Anatomy of a Murder*.

1991

Lincoln Center for the Performing Arts Inc. announces the creation of a Jazz Department with year-round programming.

Rob Gibson becomes the department's first director.

1992

Wynton Marsalis's first commissioned work for Jazz at Lincoln Center: *In This House, on This Morning*.

The Jazz at Lincoln Center Orchestra embarks on its first tour of the United States.

Jazz for Young People concerts are hosted by Wynton Marsalis and the Jazz on Film series begins.

Jazz at Lincoln Center Radio hosted by Ed Bradley begins its first season of nationally syndicated broadcasts.

1993

Jazz Talk series begins.

Jazz in the Schools tours begin.

Premiere of first major collaboration: *Jazz (Six Syncopated Movements)* with the New York City Ballet.

OPPOSITE: Jon Hendricks and Cassandra Wilson exiting the stage after a 1997 *Blood on the Fields* performance.

ABOVE: Wynton Marsalis adjusting the music during a 1993 rehearsal.

RIGHT: Sherman Irby in *God's Trombone*.

FAR RIGHT: Jared Grimes onstage at JALC.

IDENTITY 181

1994

Jazz at Lincoln Center's first appearance on PBS's *Live from Lincoln Center* broadcast.

Premiere of *Blood on the Fields* by the Jazz at Lincoln Center Orchestra with special guests Cassandra Wilson, Jon Hendricks, and Miles Griffith.

1995

First international tour of the Jazz at Lincoln Center Orchestra.

Year-round education department forms.

1996

Jazz at Lincoln Center is unanimously voted by all constituents to become the twelfth Lincoln Center constituent organization.

Gordon J. Davis is appointed chairman of the JALC Board of Directors.

First Annual Essentially Ellington High School Jazz Band Competition and Festival opens to tri-state area.

Jazz at Lincoln Center Orchestra collaborates with the Alvin Ailey American Dance Theater as part of the first Lincoln Center Festival.

1997

Wynton Marsalis is the first jazz musician to be awarded the Pulitzer Prize for Music for his Jazz at Lincoln Center–commissioned composition *Blood on the Fields*.

Jazz at Lincoln Center Radio hosted by Ed Bradley wins a Peabody Award for excellence in broadcasting.

1998

First Jazz at Lincoln Center tours to Asia, Russia, and Australia, including a weeklong residency in Yokohama, Japan.

ABOVE: Victor Goines working on the music during the 2010 Barbican Residency.

RIGHT: Reynaldo Jorge and Luis Bonilla of the Afro-Latin Jazz Orchestra, 2004.

FAR RIGHT: Wynton Marsalis writing percussion parts during a flight to Berlin for 2010's *Swing Symphony*.

1999

Jazz at Lincoln Center celebrates the Ellington Centennial with a season of music dedicated exclusively to Ellington's music. JALC expands the Essentially Ellington High School Jazz Band program to all fifty states.

On Duke's 100th birthday, JALC celebrates with a ride on the A train from Harlem to Columbus Circle with JLCO musicians performing a second line up Broadway to the Lincoln Center Plaza, where 500 Essentially Ellington alumni play Duke's "C Jam Blues." JALC publishes *Jump for Joy: Jazz at Lincoln Center Celebrates the Ellington Centennial, 1899–1999.*

John Lewis conducts the Jazz at Lincoln Center Orchestra in *Jump for Joy: John Lewis Plays Ellington.*

Premiere of *All Rise* with the Jazz at Lincoln Center Orchestra and the New York Philharmonic.

2000

First Band Director Academy, in collaboration with Jazz Aspen Snowmass, Snowmass, Colorado.

Ted Ammon is appointed chairman of the JALC Board of Directors.

The Jazz at Lincoln Center Orchestra and the New York Film Society collaborate: *Body and Soul* composed by Wycliffe Gordon.

JLCO tours take a leap forward with a tour of fifteen countries including eight multiday residencies and a swing dance tour across America.

2001

JALC publishes the first scores in the *Essential Jazz Editions* series in collaboration with the Smithsonian Institution.

United Nations Secretary General Kofi Annan proclaims Wynton Marsalis an international ambassador of goodwill by appointing him a U.N. Messenger of Peace.

JALC celebrates the Louis Armstrong Centennial with international programming and a tour with the Jazz at Lincoln Center Orchestra.

JLCO touring includes premiere of Marsalis's *Vitoria Suite* in Vitoria, Spain, and a collaboration with the Los Angeles Philharmonic performing *All Rise.*

Lisa Schiff is appointed chairman of the JALC Board of Directors following the death of Ted Ammon.

2002

JALC publishes Jazz for Young People Curriculum.

JALC launches adult education courses.

Essentially Ellington Down Under in Australia is piloted.

Board member Hughlyn F. Fierce is named president and CEO of Jazz at Lincoln Center and spearheads the construction of Frederick P. Rose Hall.

Frederick P. Rose Hall has its groundbreaking ceremony.

2003

Jazz for Young People Curriculum Online is launched.

"Jazz and American Democracy," an exploration of the impact of Jazz on American culture and politics, includes the Honorable William Jefferson Clinton, forty-second President of the United States, Wynton Marsalis, and an esteemed panel hosted by Charlie Rose. Event plants the seeds of WeBop and the study of jazz at an early age.

RIGHT: Wynton Marsalis struggling to write music in the car on another twenty-hour drive.

FAR RIGHT: Dan Nimmer, pianist, and Darin Atwater, conductor, at the rehearsal of *Abyssinian 200: A Celebration* in 2008.

2004

The legendary Dave Brubeck Octet plays selections from an original 1946 octet recording for only the second time in history.

Jazz at Lincoln Center completes a $131 million fundraising campaign and opens its new home, Frederick P. Rose Hall. The event is broadcast on *Live from Lincoln Center*.

Jazz at Lincoln Center Orchestra premieres original work *Let Freedom Swing* with revolutionary speeches read by Rev. Dr. Calvin O. Butts III, Glenn Close, Keith David, Ossie Davis, Ruby Dee, and Morgan Freeman.

Jazz at Lincoln Center Orchestra collaborates with Ken Burns and performs original music from Burns's documentary, *Unforgivable Blackness*.

First Nesuhi Ertegun Jazz Hall of Fame induction ceremony.

WeBop classes for two- to five-year-olds and their parents or caregivers begin.

2005

Max Roach and Sonny Rollins accept Nesuhi Ertegun Jazz Hall of Fame induction awards.

Frederick P. Rose Hall visitorship surpasses the 250,000 mark.

Jazz at Lincoln Center holds the Higher Ground Hurricane Relief Benefit Concert, which, along with auctions, donations, and record sales, raises funds for musicians and music-related enterprises in New Orleans.

Essentially Ellington, celebrating its tenth year, reaches more than 250,000 students and distributes over 65,000 scores.

JALC publishes first Jazz for Young People series music scores.

Random House publishes *Understanding Jazz* by Tom Piazza and Jazz at Lincoln Center.

JALC launches the Middle School Jazz Academy, offering tuition-free instrumental jazz instruction to New York City middle school students.

2006

Rose Theater and The Allen Room surpass the 500-event mark.

Jazz at Lincoln Center Orchestra and Odadaa! premiere Wynton Marsalis and Yacub Addy's *Congo Square* in Louis Armstrong Park in New Orleans in the wake of Hurricane Katrina, followed by a national tour.

NEA Jazz in the Schools Web-based curriculum launches, reaching an estimated 4.8 million students in its first year.

The Rhythm Road: American Music Abroad program launches its first tour as a partnership between the U.S. Department of State's Bureau of Educational and Cultural Affairs and JALC, marking JALC's first trip to Africa.

Essentially Ellington expands to include regional festivals across the country.

2007

Chops, a documentary featuring Essentially Ellington, premieres at New York's Tribeca Film Festival.

Jazz in the Schools' 330+ live performances reach more than 60,000 New York City students.

Jazz Education Events Online launches, bringing JALC's education programs to a world audience via the Internet.

Jazz at Lincoln Center Orchestra, in collaboration with the Museum of Modern Art, premieres *Jazz and Art: Portrait in Seven Shades*, a new commission by Ted Nash.

Celebrating 15 years, Jazz for Young People concerts reach more than 125,000 parents and children in our halls and at Harlem's Apollo Theater, while the curriculum reaches millions in the classroom and online.

Hall of Fame concert series is launched.

2008

JALC fulfills the final financial obligation on the construction of Frederick P. Rose Hall, marking its full and debt-free ownership of the facility.

JALC celebrates Abyssinian Baptist Church's bicentennial with *Abyssinian 200: A Celebration*, written by Wynton Marsalis for the JLCO and the Abyssinian Baptist Church Choir with sermon by Rev. Dr. Calvin O. Butts III.

JALC launches the content-rich Nesuhi Ertegun Jazz Hall of Fame website.

Frederick P. Rose Hall surpasses the 1 million visitors mark.

First cycle of *The Rhythm Road* program is complete, having toured to eighty-nine countries. U.S. State Department renews JALC as grant administrator.

Jazz at Lincoln Center produces nearly 3,000 events for the first time.

RIGHT: Three young girls demonstrate the freedom of expression in swinging.

FAR RIGHT: Wynton Marsalis, Rob Gibson, and Leonard Slatkin, composer, reviewing new orchestrations of Duke Ellington's *A Tone Parallel to Harlem* in 1999.

2009

Wynton Marsalis delivers the Nancy Hanks Lecture on Arts and Public Policy at the Kennedy Center—where his speech, "The Ballad of American Arts," brings a packed house of more than 2,000 to their feet for a tear-filled, ten-minute standing ovation.

In the Best Possible Light: Herman Leonard's Jazz opens in the Peter Jay Sharp Arcade, featuring more than forty iconic black and white images from the famed photographer.

Jazz at Lincoln Center celebrates the tenth anniversary of its annual Band Director Academy. Since inception, 547 band directors have attended; sixteen sessions have been held in eight locations in the United States and Canada taught by twenty faculty members on thirty-six class topics.

Michael Feinstein joins Jazz at Lincoln Center as the artistic director for the Jazz & Popular Song series.

2010

The Barbican Centre in London announces its first International Residency Series—a ten-year partnership with Jazz at Lincoln Center featuring concerts, education workshops, and master classes.

CBS's *60 Minutes* goes on the road with the Jazz at Lincoln Center Orchestra for a historic first trip to Cuba. The two-segment feature is broadcast twice and watched by millions of viewers.

Wynton Marsalis's *Swing Symphony*, a co-commission with the Berlin Philharmonic Orchestra, New York Philharmonic, Los Angeles Philharmonic, and The Barbican Centre, premieres in Berlin with the Jazz at Lincoln Center Orchestra and the Berliner Philharmoniker, led by Sir Simon Rattle.

Jazz at Lincoln Center launches *Jazz Stories*, the new podcast of Jazz at Lincoln Center Radio.

Essentially Ellington turns fifteen.

2011

Jazz at Lincoln Center forms a global partnership with Starwood to build jazz clubs in St. Regis hotels around the world.

Jazz at Lincoln Center teams up with City Center for *Cotton Club Parade*, a celebration of Ellington's years at the famed Harlem nightclub in the 1920s and early '30s, with revues featuring big bands, swing, and blues, dancers, singers, and novelty acts.

Wynton Marsalis is named CBS News Cultural Correspondent.

2012

Jazz at Lincoln Center Doha opens its doors in the new St. Regis hotel in Qatar. This is the first permanent home built by any constituent of Lincoln Center.

Lisa Schiff steps down as chairman of the Board of Directors after leading the organization since 2002. Bob Appel is named as her successor.

Jazz at Lincoln Center premieres two newly commissioned works by members of the orchestra, the spiritually focused *God's Trombones* by Chris Crenshaw and the multilayered ballet *Inferno* by Sherman Irby.

Steadfast supporters Jack and Susan Rudin commit to endowing the Essentially Ellington Program. This is the first program of Jazz at Lincoln Center to ever be endowed.

Jazz at Lincoln Center celebrates twenty-five years as an institution.

LEFT: Arturo O'Farrill, pianist, and a Ballet Hispanico dancer, Frederick P. Rose Hall, 2006.

ABOVE RIGHT: Audience at a 2000 performance.

PREVIOUS PAGE: A little trumpet player, Jeff, playing a tune for JLCO members, 2006.

LEFT: Jennifer Sanon, vocalist, Joe Saylor, drummer, and Jonathan Batiste, pianist, Dizzy's Club Coca-Cola, 2010.

BELOW, LEFT: Cécile McLorin Salvant, 2012.

BELOW, CENTER: Ulysses Owens Jr., Dizzy's Club Coca-Cola, 2012.

BELOW, RIGHT: Cedar Walton, pianist, and Roy Hargrove, trumpeter, at the Allen Room, 2009.

OPPOSITE: Wynton Marsalis and Benny Carter deep into the score.

SWING PROVIDES THE OPPORTUNITY TO CELEBRATE AN EVER-PRESENT freedom of choice.

Swinging challenges us to use that freedom to make adjustments for the common good. And making adjustments is not considered a problem. The act of adjusting, with style and playful action, is the substance of jazz itself. When well played, this music exemplifies the triumph of reason over immediacy and, through playing the blues, the victory of good times over bad.

Jazz music points us in the ascendant direction of our finest inclinations. If we, at Jazz at Lincoln Center, can grow our community through illuminating the democratic spirit of our music in the broadest social context, we will have achieved our highest aspiration. We seek to present this music in its most potent form: in the concert hall, in church, in the club, on the dance floor, at a picnic, a parade, and anywhere else folks congregate to have a good time. This music is capable of telling us who we are, where we are, where we have been, and what we must do in order to be where we want to be—which is somewhere that improvising, swinging, and playing the blues is recognized, regenerated, and respected.

In the early years, when we saw the expenses for the big band, some of us wanted to abandon it and feature small groups. Ahmet Ertegun gave an impassioned affirmation of the power and poetry of the large ensemble. He evoked the memory of the great Afro-American orchestras he and his brother, Nesuhi, heard when they first came to America. "That sound," he said, "should never be allowed to die. We must keep a sitting orchestra or this is not worth doing." On another occasion, when we saw the costs of the radio show, we wanted to cut it. I remember when Rob Gibson first talked about the show's reach and impact. "We're going to play the concert either way. You'd rather reach 2,000 or 200,000?" The general feeling: "Who listens to jazz radio anyway? Let's cut it."

MICHAEL MWENSO
VOCALIST, CURATOR/
PROGRAMMING ASSOCIATE
JAZZ AT LINCOLN CENTER

AS A YOUNG BOY GROWING UP IN LONDON,

I would wait every week with excitement to hear the live broadcasts on *Jazz at Lincoln Center Radio*. Since these musicians rarely performed in London, the radio shows were a lifeline. Every note, every shout chorus, every solo brought me closer to the epicenter of jazz: New York City.

It was a great thrill to hear masters such as John Lewis, Frank Wess, Joe Henderson, and an eighty-three-year-old Benny Carter playing with such zeal and vigor alongside our younger musicians like Christian McBride, Marcus Roberts, and Roy Hargrove. When great musicians of different generations play with a mutual depth and spiritual engagement, it is reminiscent of the best moments of days past (like when Coleman Hawkins, a grandmaster, would play with a newcomer like Miles Davis).

The work of Jazz at Lincoln Center has allowed me to grasp the holistic nature of this music. It has shown me that there is no generation gap, no division by race or ethnicity, and no judgment of one's self, at which point we are, indeed, united in swing.

THE SIXTH GIG IN FIVE DAYS. WE ARE BONE TIRED. DOES IT MAKE a difference? We're not leading the nation in digital downloads, there's no jazz on television, we have an aging audience. Why are we out here? We just played a two-hour gig, there is another ten-plus-hour drive tonight, and about thirty-seven people, two busloads of kids, and their directors and chaperones are backstage waiting for autographs and lessons. It's already 11 P.M., the car is leaving at 1 A.M., and the people are ready to close the Hall and go home.

JONO GASPARRO
MANAGER, RESEARCH AND NEW INITIATIVES-EDUCATION
JAZZ AT LINCOLN CENTER

AS A STUDENT GROWING UP IN OHIO, I would

take "sick days" from school and drive for hours with friends to see the Jazz at Lincoln Center Orchestra with Wynton Marsalis. This annual excursion was our chance to hear the music we loved performed at the highest level, and it provided an opportunity to speak with band members and interact with the music on a more social level. They were our heroes and very approachable.

One fall evening in Ann Arbor, Michigan, thanks to Wess "Warmdaddy" Anderson, we made it backstage after a concert. Being a trumpet player, I was anxiously standing in line to say something inconsequential to Wynton, while Carlos Henriquez taught a friend how to double stop on the bass, and another friend, a pianist, went searching for Eric Lewis. To my surprise, Wynton and some of the band (the rest went to go play a jam session with local students) stayed at Hill Auditorium well past midnight. Standing there, I was ignorant of the history of the JLCO and the tradition it embodied.

I had no idea that Dizzy Gillespie once told Wynton to keep the band going even if he didn't want to, because losing our orchestral music would be a national disgrace, or that my own high school jazz teacher, Todd Stoll, had once been my age waiting backstage to shake Mr. Gillespie's hand.

Eight years after that autumn evening in Michigan, I found myself traveling some American highway sleeping in the "junk bunk" on the JLCO tour bus. My road jobs included pulling luggage from underneath the buses with veteran road warrior Frank Stewart, making sure the coffee was hot, and assisting Boss Murphy in "band member counting." But the most instructional job of all took place after the stage was dark. I would stay after every show and watch Wynton greet every single child, father, mother, music teacher, retiree, student, clergyman, jazz fan, mayor, and journalist. And though each individual interaction was relatively short, I could see that they were truly powerful.

Those ninety-minute concerts, followed by an iPhone photo, a lesson, some autographs, or just a handshake in Mobile, Akron, Carmel, or Philadelphia, were reaffirmations of the basic truth of jazz: It's personal.

It will have a lasting impact. Actually, I strongly believe it.

TOP, LEFT: Roy Haynes, 2011.

TOP, RIGHT: Harlem Boys Choir, 2006.

FAR LEFT: Roy Haynes's grandson, Marcus Gilmore, in 2004.

LEFT: Wynton Marsalis playing with a finalist band on the ending night of Essentially Ellington.

ABOVE: Carlos Henriquez and Joe Temperley as a four-armed tick, as Kenny Rampton looks on.

OPPOSITE: Saxophonists Stacy Dillard and Marcus Strickland.

WE HAVE A SAYING: "LET'S GET OUT THERE." That means, make something happen. On the road, it's easy to stay in the hotel to conserve energy for the night. But when you do get out there, you never know what wonderful moments are waiting for you.

MARCUS PRINTUP
TRUMPETER, JAZZ AT LINCOLN CENTER ORCHESTRA

WE WERE IN SEATTLE ON TOUR,

and a high school band that I mentored at our Essentially Ellington festival invited me and three other cats from the band (Wess Anderson, Walter Blanding, Andre Hayward) to conduct a morning master class. After the class, the director, Jake Bergevin, told us that the great saxophonist Lucky Thompson was in a nursing home outside of Seattle. We had a few hours before sound check, so we asked to be driven there. The workers at the home knew nothing of Lucky's artistry. They told us that he had Alzheimer's and hadn't spoken a word in years.

I remember entering this large room with an old man sitting in a green recliner. It was Lucky. Wess was our spokesperson and introduced us all. Even with Wess's soulful personality, Lucky didn't respond and looked at us like we were crazy. We then decided that we'd just play for him and leave him be. We played "Parker's Mood." Wess played the intro and I swear to you Lucky's eyes opened so wide. We all took a chorus, and on each chorus, Lucky came more and more alive. After a few minutes, the room was full of other residents of the home.

When we finished, Lucky looked up and said, "Man, where's my horn?" He came alive and was conversing with us as if we were in a jazz club. "Where you all from? New York? How is ole Clark Terry doing? How about Al Grey? You all sure sound good. Play something else!"

We played for about forty-five minutes. It was incredible.

BELOW: Barry Harris teaching students of Middle School Jazz Academy, 2007.

OPPOSITE: Ben Wolfe, pianist, with Billy Banks and a group of children.

OPPOSITE, RIGHT: Wynton Jr. and Simeon Marsalis supporting their father during a rehearsal in 1992.

DAVE BERGER WAS THE FIRST CONDUCTOR OF THE JAZZ AT Lincoln Center Orchestra. We have been adjudicating bands for all seventeen years of the Essentially Ellington Festival. It never gets old. We call the kids "our" or "my" on the judging sheets. "Our" trombone section needs better intonation, or "my" little red-haired bassist is swinging, or I love "our" clarinet. Dave believes this music can affect positive change in our way of life.

DAVID BERGER
ARRANGER
ESSENTIALLY ELLINGTON

ONCE, ABOUT THIRTY YEARS AGO,

I was in a hotel lobby in Italy at the ungodly hour of five o'clock in the morning. I saw a man happily sweeping the floor. As he swept, he sang one of my favorite Verdi arias. One day I hope that all Americans will similarly embrace our great heritage and truly know who we are.

THE MOST MOVING PERFORMANCE WE HAVE HEARD OVER the seventeen years of Essentially Ellington was Hall High School's in 1998. This young lady played "Prelude to a Kiss," then led her saxophone section in the difficult sax soli of Duke Ellington's "Cottontail" from memory. We all erupted in ecstasy and knew then that this program was having an impact.

ERICA VON KLEIST
SAXOPHONIST, FORMER ESSENTIALLY ELLINGTON PARTICIPANT

JAZZ AT LINCOLN CENTER HAS ALWAYS STOOD BY A STEADY PHILOSOPHY.

Jazz swings. Jazz has blues. Jazz is a musical language that has remained true to its traditions while still evolving throughout a century of history. In my short career I have had the opportunity to be a part of this tradition, and much of my experience has been through Jazz at Lincoln Center.

For me, it began in high school, as a member of the Hall High School Concert Jazz Band, performing at the Essentially Ellington Festival. Four years in a row, the band covered some of the greatest music ever written, which in itself is an education to last a lifetime, let alone competing against some of the country's most talented young people, all vying for accolades from Wynton, Michael Brecker, David Sanborn, and countless other jazz greats who judged the bands.

My inspiration to move to New York came from having been exposed to great jazz at a young age, and the energy and soul therein. Since then, I have partaken in almost every aspect of Jazz at Lincoln Center, as a graduate of the Juilliard Jazz program, to being a touring member of the JLCO. I have also worked as a mentor for the Essentially Ellington Festival and performed at Dizzy's Club with my groups. Jazz at Lincoln Center has become like a second home for me.

What draws people to want to be a part of Jazz at Lincoln Center is its consistency. Audiences at Rose Hall know they're going to hear a class act, swinging, high-quality performance by a seasoned group of masters. However, several critics have argued that since Jazz at Lincoln Center is funded partly by public monies, it should reflect all aspects of society, often alluding to the fact that there isn't a woman in the band. They question why a racially diverse orchestra who is represented by musicians of all ages can't include at least one female. Since public tax money is partially contributing to the institution's success, shouldn't it provide equal opportunity to musicians of all races, backgrounds, and genders?

When it comes to choosing musicians for an ensemble, bandleaders often consider a number of factors. Is this person punctual? Do they jibe well with the other band members? Can they play all the instruments the music requires? Depending on the gig, factors like gender, body type, and other superficial qualities may come into play. Do they look good in the costumes? Can they dance? Sometimes bandleaders do in fact hire a musician based on gender. There are all-female bands in existence where the number one prerequisite is obviously the fact that the members are women. Every bandleader has his or her own priorities when forming an ensemble, and each priority is valid. To each his own.

OPPOSITE: Saxophonists Erica von Kleist and Joe Temperley during the 1999 Essentially Ellington competition.

BELOW: McCoy Tyner, pianist, and Ravi Coltrane, tenor saxophonist, at the Allen Room, 2009.

BOTTOM: Wynton Guess, center, learning blues chords with André Guess, left, Walter Blanding, Kwami Coleman, Raymond Murphy, Herlin Riley, and Eric Lewis, 2003.

BOTTOM, RIGHT: The finale in the fabled *Palau de la Música* in Valencia, Spain, 2009.

I know that in the past I have been hired because of my gender. Rarely do I ever escape a performance where someone in the audience approaches me, applauding my resolve to become a jazz musician despite the fact that I am a woman. Quite honestly, I don't actually know what it feels like to be a female jazz musician, simply because I've never been a man.

Wynton has always chosen his band members very carefully. In his groups, the absolute first requirement of all the musicians is "Can he or she swing?" This is by far the most crucial factor in determining if someone is right for the band, and has been since Jazz at Lincoln Center started twenty-five years ago. The orchestra is composed of some of the most gifted, talented, knowledgeable, and, yes, swinging jazz musicians alive. Each member has earned a spot in the band, not because he was born looking a certain way, but because he has studied the music and has an innate gift of executing it with the soul and feeling appropriate for the Jazz at Lincoln Center Orchestra. Diversity is alive and well in the band, not due to strategy, but due to happenstance. I too have had the privilege of performing and touring with the band, and I just happen to be female. I most certainly prefer it this way, because I know I'm hired based upon merit, not on my appearance. This makes me proud because I worked a lot harder to become an accomplished musician than I did to become a female.

The tide of public opinion ebbs and flows. Some institutions have proven to be malleable in their philosophies, bending whenever a negatively tinged article is published, or if a prominent funder expresses distaste with a decision. Music is first and foremost at Jazz at Lincoln Center—it is the creed on which the establishment is based. If other ideals supersede those that make the music great, then the foundation on which Jazz at Lincoln Center stands becomes compromised. For twenty-five years, Jazz at Lincoln Center has brought jazz, swinging jazz, to the masses. Consistency has been the key to its success, and it's what its structure is built upon. This has been the mission since the beginning, and this is why Jazz at Lincoln Center is, and will always be, the House of Swing.

LEGACY 195

MANY THINGS DON'T LAST LONG IN AMERICA.

GREG SCHOLL
EXECUTIVE DIRECTOR
JAZZ AT LINCOLN CENTER

As a culture, we passionately embrace something, throw ourselves into it wholeheartedly, poke, prod, and experiment…until we cast it away for the new. This quality makes America a dynamic place full of promise, possibility, curiosity, and restless movement—and contributes to our uniquely powerful economy and the awe-inspiring pace of our technological change. There's a lot to be said for how we roll.

However, towering genius walked our recent cultural path, staking out dynamic new music forms and means of expression. Innovators like Morton, Armstrong, Ellington, Parker, and Monk left bodies of work that deserve the level of respect and focused exploration that we give to other vaunted musical arts, classical and otherwise.

This is what we, at Jazz at Lincoln Center, do.

Forward momentum in jazz is unstoppable, but music that swings deserves a permanent home—our home, the House of Swing. The music we serve merits this home. Our music has inherent aesthetic value and vital, contemporary cultural relevance.

If we were to think about Jazz at Lincoln Center as a hierarchy, all of us, down here at the bottom of the pyramid, throw ourselves into our work and do our jobs well. One level above is a belief we all share: that this specific music we serve merits the physical and spiritual home we give it, and not only can we be successful by focusing on it but, in the long term, our success can come in no other way—like any other organization, there is beauty, power, and magic in focus. Finally, there is a top to this pyramid, which is our most enlightened belief: that this specific music has the power to raise the consciousness of our country, culture, and kids.

This draws us together here—our diverse staff, our remarkable artists, our committed trustees, our other valued financial supporters. A person catching a Rose Hall performance or a late-night set at Dizzy's, a WeBop class, or an Essentially Ellington competition.

It is an honor for all of us to serve our music and our mission. This document of JALC's first twenty-five years is an astonishing reminder of the audacity of its vision and the profound dedication, hard work, and creative problem-solving of the founding team. May we draw inspiration from it, and may the next twenty-five years be as fruitful and fun as the ones that came before.

OPPOSITE, TOP: Second line at Lionel Hampton's funeral, 2002.

OPPOSITE, BOTTOM: *Higher Ground* finale, 2005.

INDEX

A

Abdul-Jabbar, Kareem, 95
Abyssinian Baptist Church, 55, 184
Addy, Yacub, 39, 141, 151, 171, 184
Adler, Nick, 136
Adnet, Mario, 151
African Rhythms Orchestra, 47
Afro-Latin Jazz Orchestra, *98*, 99, 150, *153*, *182*
Akiyoshi, Toshiko, 99, 171
Al-Alami, Zak, 135
Alexander, Monty, *58*, 59, 151
Alice Tully Hall, 15, 16, 17, 18–19, 23, 30, 31, 32, 33, 34, 36, 47, 77, 141, 151, 176
Allen, Geri, 151, 171
Allen, Herb, 96
Allen, Woody, 157, 171
Allen Room, 85, 88, 96, *154–55*, 156
Alvin Ailey American Dance Theater, 29, 64, 171, 182
American Composers Orchestra, 171
Ammon, Ted, *82*, 92, 96, 183
Anderson, Ernestine, 19
Anderson, Wess "Warmdaddy," 19, *28*, 29, 36, 55, 114, 122, 125, 151, *168*, 169, *170*, 177, 190, 192
Andrade, Leny, 36
Anka, Paul, 171
Annan, Kofi, 183
Apollo Theater, 55, 159, 184
Appel, Helen, *131*
Appel, Robert, *131*, 185
Arana, Lauren, 134
Armacost, Tim, 171
Armand, Gabrielle, 134
Armstrong, Louis, 20, 22, 39, 63, 67, 88, 96, 105, 151, 157, 169, 183, 197

Arnhold, John, 150, 168
Arrendell, Ed, 141
Ashby, Harold, 151
Ashley, Dwayne, 134
Aslan, Pablo, 171
Atwater, Darin, 171, *183*
Auer, Bob, 136
Austin, Patti, 171
Avery Fisher Hall, 45, 46, 62, 68, 71, 151, 158
Awards, 161

B

Bacher, Kurt, 171
Baeza, Mario, 22
Ballet Hispanico, 150, *185*
Band Director Academy, 68, 183, 185
Banks, Billy, *114*, 115, 135, 136, 192, *193*
Barbican Centre, 64, 185
Barkan, Todd, 134, 142, 179
Barker, Danny, 19
Baron, Art, 18, 19
Barron, Farid, 117
Barron, Kenny, 18, 151
Bartlett, Jennifer, 159
Bartley, Patrick, 70, 71
Basie, Count, 168
Batiste, Alvin, 19
Batiste, Jonathan, 75, *188*
Bauzá, Mario, 36
Beiderbecke, Bix, 169
Belgrave, Marcus, 18, 19, 105, *115*
Benn, Randy, *82*
Bennett, Tony, 59, 99, 151, 157
Benson, George, 171
Berger, David, 18, 19, *29*, 31, 68, 171, 181, 193
Bergevin, Jake, 192
Berkow, Sam, 89
Berlin Philharmonic Orchestra, 59, 150, 185
Bernstein, Leonard, 44
Best, Ravi, 62
Biasetti, Bob, 135
Birnbaum, Adam, 76
Blakey, Art, 178
Blanding, Walter, *10*, 11, *108*, 110, 122, 123, 125, 171, 192, *195*
Blind Boys of Alabama, 171
Bloom, Harold, 20
Bloomberg, Michael, 96
Bloomgarden, Alina, *15*, *16*, 20, 29, 152, 181
Blue Note Records, 144
Bly, Vincent, 136, 179
Body and Soul (film), 151, 183
Bonilla, Luis, *182*
Bradley, Ed, *46*, 151, 158, 161, 171, 181, 182
Bravo, Luis, 134
Brecker, Michael, 194
Bridgewater, Dee Dee, 171
Brown, Ray, *17*, 19, *32*, 75
Brown, Ruth, 157, 171
Brubeck, Dave, 151, 184
Bryant, Ray, 18
Buffett, Jimmy, 157, 159, 171
Bunge, Greg, 72
Burke, Geoff, 110
Burns, Ken, *148*, 161, 184
Burrell, Kim, 171
Butcher, William, 22
Butman, Igor, *34*, 99, 141
Butts, Calvin O., III, 184

Butts, Tiffany Ellis, 54, 55
Byard, Jaki, 18
Byars, Chris, 171
Byrd, Donald, 19

C

Cachaito, 151
Caesar, Shirley, 55, 145
Callaway, Ann Hampton, 171
Camilo, Michel, 36, 171
Campbell, Mary Schmidt, 22
Carnegie Hall Jazz Band, 151
Carroll, Diahann, 171
Carroll Music Studios, 166
Carter, Benny, 16, 17, 19, *35*, 78, 161, 171, 176, 188, 189, *189*
Carter, Betty, *16*, 18, 47, 151, 171, 176
Carter, Regina, 171
Carter, Ron, 19, *23*, 47
Cedric the Entertainer, 159, 171
Chait, Orin, 134, 135
Chamber Music Society of Lincoln Center, *44–45*, 53
Chambers, Joe, 171
Changuito, 151
Chapman, Tracy, 159, 171
Charlap, Bill, *40*, 99, 171
Charlap, Moose, 40
Charlap, Tom, 40
Charles, Ray, 157, 159, 170, 171
Chase, Chevy, 159, 171
Chassagne, Roland, 94–95
Cheadle, Don, 159, 171
Cheatham, Doc, 18
Childs, Billy, 171
Chops (film), 68, 184
Chorale Le Chateau, 151

Chuffo, Paul, 47
City Center Encores!, 64
Clapton, Eric, *156*, 157, 159, 170, 171, *177*
Clark, John, 19
Clark, Thais, 19
Clinton, Bill, 183
Clinton, Hillary, *82*
Close, Glenn, 145, 184
Cocker, Joe, 159, 171
Coffey, Diane, 22, 53, 179
Cohn, Alan, 53, 168
Cole, Natalie, 171
Coleman, Earl, 18
Coleman, George, 18
Coleman, Kwami, *195*
Coleman, Ornette, 20, 95, 151
Colina, Annie, 36
Coltrane, John, 33, 34, 99, 126
Coltrane, Ravi, *195*
Columbia Records, 85
Columbia University, 79
Columbus Youth Jazz Orchestra, 76
Congo Square, 39, 144, 184
Connaughton, Artie, 141
Connick, Harry, Jr., 18, *158*
Cook, Barbara, 171
Cook, Willie, 18, 19
Cooper, Buster, 18, 19
Corea, Chick, 151, 179
Cosby, Bill, *98*, 99, 145, 157, 176
Crawford, Stacie Middleton, 136
Crenshaw, Chris, 75, 78, *116*, 117, *124*, 126, 151, 171, 185
Crouch, Stanley, 16, *20*, 22, 29, 30, 53, 169, 176, 181
Cruz, Celia, 36, *37*, 151
Cuscuna, Michael, 144

D

Daltonn, Sasha, 18
Dameron, Tadd, 18
Dameronia, 18
David, Keith, 184
Davis, Gordon, 22, 23, 29, 30, 50, 53, 83, 85, 92, 96, 105, 131, 161, 181, 182
Davis, Miles, 34, 85, 105, 168, 189
Davis, Ossie, 184
Davis, Walter, Jr., 16, 18, 19
Dee, Ruby, 184
DeRosa, Richard, 171
De Shields, André, 53, 171
Diamond, Irene, 50, 96, 161
Diehl, Aaron, 75, 76, 77, *98*, 100
Dizzy's Club Coca-Cola, 46, 47, 85, 88, *89*, 95, 96, *98*, 141, 142, 152, *188*, 194
Djangirov, Eldar, 171
Dr. John, 171
Dodgion, Jerry, *178*
Dominguez, Chano, 141, 151, 171
Donaldson, Lou, 159, 171
Dorham, Kenny, 168
Doria, Damian, 89
Dorsey, Christopher, 71
Downey, Robert, Jr., 159, 171
D'Rivera, Paquito, 36, *37*, 99, 171
Drummond, Anne, 171
Drummond, Ray, 19
Durham, Bobby, 19
Dylan, Bob, 85, *156*, 157, 159, 171

E

Easley, Bill, *28*, 29
Ed Bradley Award, 158, 161

Edison, Harry "Sweets," 16, *17*, 18
Elgort, Arthur, 15, 20, *175*
Ellington, Duke, 15, 16, 18, 19, 29, 34, 55, 68, 72, 105, 117, 126, 150, 151, 168, 169, 170, 176, 181, 183, 185, 197
Ellis, Arlise, 134
Emilio, Frank, 151
Empire State Building, *179*
English, Christi, 110, 135
Epstein, Steve, 89, 119
Ertegun, Ahmet, 22, 96, 161, 189
Ertegun, Nesuhi, 96, 189
Ertegun Jazz Hall of Fame, *88*, 89, 96, 184
Essentially Ellington program, *60–61*, 62, 66, 67, 68, *69–71*, 72, 74, 75, 76, 77, 78, 182, 183, 184, 185, 193, 194
Evans, Gil, 85, 151

F

Faddis, Jon, *178*
Fagan, Garth, 99
Fantasia, *160*, 171
Farber, Andy, 171
Farinacci, Dominick, 75
Farmer, Art, 19, 171
Farrante, Frank, 141
Feinstein, Michael, 171, 185
Felder, Marion, 75
Feldstein, Sandy, 67
Feliciano, Brenda, 36, *37*
Fiance, Mary, 134, 175–76, 179
Fierce, Hughlyn, 53, 94–95, 161, *168*, 169, 183
Film Society of Lincoln Center, 151
Fishburne, Laurence, 145, *148*, 159, 171

Flack, Roberta, 171
Flamenco Jazz Ensemble, 151
Flanagan, Tommy, 16, 18, 19, 171
Fleming, Renée, *147*
Floreska, Erika, 68
Foster, Frank, 171
Franceschini, Bob, 171
Franklin, Aretha, *156*, 157, 171
Frederick P. Rose Hall, 85, 88–89, *90–91*, 94, 97, 99, *100–101*, *136–37*, 143, 183, 184
Freeman, Morgan, 184
Freeman, Von, 19
Fricklas, Michael, 53
Frissell, Bill, 171
Fruit, Chuck, 96
Fuller, Curtis, 19

G

Galas, *154–56*, 157, *158–61*, 171
Gardner, Earl, 19
Gardner, Vincent, *116*, *122*, 141, 150, 171, *172–73*, 175, *178*, 179
Gasparro, Jono, 190
George, Nathan, 119
Gershwin, George, 45
Gibson, David, 144, 181, *184*
Gibson, Rob, 29, 30, 31, 44, 47, 50, 83, *88*, 89, 92, 189
Gillespie, Dizzy, 16, *17*, 19, 33, 34, 126, 168, 190
Gilmore, Marcus, 171, *191*
Giuliani, Rudy, 85, 96, 175
Givey, Michael, 134
Glover, Savion, 99, 159, 171
Goines, Victor, *28*, 29, 56, 67, 75, 76, 110, 119, 123, 141, 159, 169, *170*, 171, *182*

INDEX

Goldberg, Whoopi, 159, 171

Golson, Benny, 19, 75, 171

Goodman, Benny, 98

Gordon, Dexter, 18

Gordon, Lorraine, 161

Gordon, Wycliffe, 26, 29, 98, 104, 105, 112–13, 115, 122, 151, 159, 171, 178, 183

Gould, Glenn, 85

Graham, Julia, 135

Granz, Norman, 161

Graves, Denyce, 171

Grayson, Milt, 29, 97, 105, 116, 117, 171, 176

Gregory, Ernie, 136

Grey, Al, 26, 29, 107

Griffin, Johnny, 16, 19

Griffith, Miles, 182

Grimes, Jared, 151

Grooms, James, 134

Grossman, David, 54

Guess, André, 144, 195

Guess, Wynton, 195

Gumbel, Roberta, 171

H

Haberman, Sarah, 134

Hamilton, Jimmy, 18, 19, 23, 150

Hampton, Lionel, 35, 161, 197

Hampton, Slide, 19, 27, 29, 99, 171

Hancock, Herbie, 145

Handy, W. C., 45

Hanna, Sir Roland, 19, 117, 159, 171, 174, 175

Hargrove, Roy, 171, 188, 189

Harlem Boys Choir, 191

Harris, Austin, 110, 135

Harris, Barry, 14, 15, 16, 18, 19, 171, 192

Harris, Jackie, 141

Harris, Stefon, 53, 171

Hart, Kitty Carlisle, 171

Hawkins, Coleman, 189

Haynes, Roy, 16, 18, 171, 176, 191

Hayward, Andre, 76, 77, 192

Healey, John, 135

Heath, Jimmy, 19, 24, 25, 32, 33, 171

Heath, Percy, 18, 32, 33

Heath, Tootie, 32, 33

Henderson, Joe, 18, 19, 33, 171, 176, 189

Hendricks, Jon, 16, 18, 19, 32, 59, 180, 181, 182

Henriquez, Carlos, 77, 78, 96, 109, 171, 190, 191

Henry, Cat, 134, 135

Herwig, Conrad, 171

Hicks, Naeemah, 135, 136

Higgins, Billy, 18, 19

Higher Ground Hurricane Relief Benefit Concert, 138–39, 141, 145–49, 184

Hill, Buck, 19

Hinton, Milt, 18

Hirsch, Phil, 135

Holiday, Billie, 19, 24, 151

Holland, Dave, 171

Hollywood Bowl, 31, 118, 120, 121

Horn, Shirley, 16, 19, 161, 171

Hosney, Doug, 135

Hubbard, Freddie, 171, 176

Hurricane Katrina, 143, 144, 145, 184

Hutcherson, Bobby, 19

Hutton, Barbara, 168

I

Ingram, James, 171

Irabagon, Jon, 75

Irby, Sherman, 28, 29, 110, 125, 126, 151, 171, 185

Irwin, Dennis, 19

Israels, Chuck, 171

J

Jackson, Ali, 109, 110, 123, 124, 150, 156, 171

Jackson, Mahalia, 55

Jackson, Milt, 19, 35

Jacobi, Bobby, 141

Jacobs, Phoebe, 55, 67, 141, 161

Jacquet, Illinois, 161, 176

Jarreau, Al, 159, 171

Jazz at Lincoln Center (JALC)

awards, 161

basic components of, 24

board of, 128–29, 131, 132–33

commissioned or premiered compositions and arrangements, 171

concert lists, 18, 151

founding of, 15–16, 20, 22, 24, 181

galas, 154–56, 157, 158–61, 171

as Lincoln Center constituent, 50, 53, 83, 175, 182

production process for, 134–36

on the radio, 46–47, 181, 182, 189

statistics about, 170

street view of, 80–81

timeline, 181–85

visitors services at, 152

Jazz at Lincoln Center Orchestra (JLCO)

collaborations, 58–59

formation of, 181

in performance, 31, 42–43, 45, 66, 67, 77, 100–101, 106–7, 123, 136–37, 140, 156, 158, 160–63, 177, 195

recordings, 170

on tour, 31, 114, 118–19, 125, 176, 181, 182, 183

Vogue photo shoot, 12–13, 15, 20, 21, 175

Jazz Cultural Theatre, 15

Jazz Education Events Online, 184

Jazz for Young People, 10, 11, 44, 63, 67, 75, 77, 98, 151, 181, 183, 184

Jazz in the Schools, 63, 181, 184

Jazz 101, 201, 301 classes, 63, 78

Jeffrey, Paul, 171

Jobim, Antônio Carlos, 36

John, Susan, 119, 125, 144

Johnson, James P., 47

Johnson, James Weldon, 151

Johnson, J. J., 18

Johnson, Lamont, 135

Johnson, Laura, 64, 67

Johnson, Russell, 89, 90

Jones, Etta, 19

Jones, Hank, 16, 18, 19, 75, 171

Jones, Norah, 145

Jones, Thad, 141

Jones, Tom, 159, 171

Jones, Virgil, 18

Jones, Zooey, 134, 135

Jordan, Clifford, 18

Jorge, Reynaldo, 182

Judd, Wynonna, 159, 171

Juilliard Jazz Orchestra, 46, 47

Juilliard School, 44, 46, 74–75, 76, 194

K

Kahle, Laura, 171

Kandel, Kris, 135

Kelly, Jonathan, 110, 135

Keough, Don, 96

Khan, Chaka, 171

King, B. B., *156*, 159, 171

Kirk, Dorthaan, *16*

Kisor, Ryan, *110*, 122, 125

Kitt, Eartha, 171

Knepper, Jimmy, 18, 19

Knight, Gladys, 171

Krall, Diana, 171

Kravitz, Lenny, 159, 171

Krishnamsetty, Meena, 63

Kronos Quartet, 171

Kuehn, Phil, 75

L

Laine, Dame Cleo, 171

Lalli, Sara, 134

Lander, Katie, 134

Landrieu, Mitch, 145

Lansbury, Angela, 171

Larkin, June Noble, 22, 93, 96, 161

Lecuona, Ernesto, 36

Lee, Jae K., 134

Lee, Tom, 95

LeFevre-Snee, Rachel, 135

Legend, John, 157, 159, 171

Leibovitz, Annie, 175

Leonard, Herman, 185

Leslie, Michael, 135

Leventhal, Nat, 15, 22, 30, 50, *51*, 53, 161, 181

Lewis, Cher, 169

Lewis, Ed, 53

Lewis, Eric, 190, *195*

Lewis, John, *28*, 29, 34, *35*, 47, 141, 151, 161, 166, *167*, 178, 183, 189

Lincoln, Abbey, 16, 18, 19, 24, 25, 145, 151, 179

Lincoln Center Institute, 44

Lindner, Jason, 171

Liston, Melba, 47

London Philharmonic Orchestra, 121

Lonzo, Fred, 19

Los Angeles Philharmonic, 118, 183, 185

Louis Armstrong Educational Foundation, 67, 96

Lovano, Joe, 75, *95*, *160*, 171

Lovett, Lyle, 159, 171

Luciano, Ken, 135

Lumpress, Nicole, 134

Lund, Lage, 75

LuPone, Patti, 171

M

Ma, Yo-Yo, 95

Mac, Bernie, 159, 171

Machito, 36

Madera, Jose, 171

Mahogany, Kevin, 151

Manhattan Transfer, 18

Marsalis, Branford, 151, 159, *160*, 171

Marsalis, Ellis, 75, 122

Marsalis, Wynton, 15–16, 18, 19, 22, *28*, 29, 33, 36, 39, *40–41*, 44, 45, 46, 47, 50, 53, 54, 59, 66, 67, 76, *82*, 83, *86–88*, 89, 93, 97, *104*, 105, 109, *110*, 115, 117, 118, *124*, 141, *142*, 150, *156*, 159, 169, 170, 171, 176–77, *178*, 179, *181–84*, 185, *189*, 190, 192, *193*, 195

Marshall, Tony, 22

Martins, Peter, 46

Mason, Elliot, 122

Masur, Kurt, 46, *47*, 56, 57

Mayer, John, 157, 159, 171

McBride, Christian, 171, 189

McDonald, Audra, 159, 171

McFerrin, Bobby, 171

McGee, Mary Beth, 135

McGibbon, Andy, 134

McLean, Jackie, 19

McLorin-Salvant, Cécile, *188*

McNair, Krystal, 62

McPartland, Marian, 16, 18, 171

McPherson, Charles, 18, 171

McRae, Carmen, 16, 18

McShann, Jay, 18, 151

Mehldau, Brad, 45

Melendez, Indio, 136

Merchant, Natalie, 157, 159, 171

Metropolitan Opera, 50

Meyer, Edgar, 53

Micheaux, Oscar, 151

Middle School Jazz Academy, 62, 63, 184, *192*

Militello, Bobby, 151

Mingus, Charles, 105, 170

Minnelli, Liza, *161*, 171

Mitchell, Brian Strokes, 171

Modern Jazz Quartet, 151, 166, 168

Monk, Thelonious, 18, 164, 197

Moody, James, 176

Moran, Jason, 171

Morgan, Frank, 18

Morgan State Choir, 56

Morrison, Toni, 145, *146*

Morton, Jelly Roll, 16, 19, 45, 47, 151, 197

Mossman, Michael Philip, 171

Mraz, George, 18

Mulligan, Gerry, 23, 47, 151, 171

Murphy, Raymond, 119, *195*

Murray, Albert, 22, *24*, 53, 55, 105, 161, 181

Museum of Modern Art, 108, 151, 184

Mwenso, Michael, 189

N

Nadler, Jerry, 99

Nakamura, Yasushi, 75

Nash, Dick, 122

Nash, Lewis, 151

Nash, Ted, 67, *108*, *110*, 122, 126, 136, 151, 171, *179*, 184

National Public Radio, 46–47

Nelson, Oliver, 99

Nelson, Steve, 151

Nelson, Willie, 141, *156*, 157, 159, 170, 171

Neville, Aaron, *149*

New York City Ballet, 44, 46, 52, 53, 55, 175, 181

New York Film Society, 183

New York Philharmonic, *42–43*, 44, 45, 46, 50, *54*, 55, *56–57*, 185

New York Times, 16, 31, 125, 159, 175, 179

Nichols, James, 135

INDEX

Niewood, Kay, 110, 134, 135
Nimmer, Dan, 78, *120*, 121, *177*, *179*, *183*
Norman, Jessye, 157, 171

O

O'Connor, Mark, 99, 141, *147*, 151
Odadaa!, *38*, 39, 123, 141, 151, 184
O'Day, Anita, 16, 18
O'Farrill, Arturo, *98*, 99, 150, 171, *185*
O'Farrill, Chico, 36, 150, 161, 171
Olaine, Jason, 134
Oliver, King, 16
Olstead, Reneé, 171
Oquendo, Steven, 109
Orchestra of St. Luke's, 171
Ordway Theatre, 64
Ostwald, David, 107
Owens, Ulysses, 75, *188*

P

Palmieri, Eddie, 157
Parisi, Grace, 135
Parker, Charlie, 16, 18, 34, 105, 126, 168, 197
Pascoal, Hermeto, 99
Payne, Cecil, 18
Payton, Nicholas, 36, 171
Payton, Walter, 19
Perez, Danilo, 171
Person, Houston, 19
Peterson, Oscar, 161
Peyroux, Madeline, 151
Piazza, Tom, 184
Piazzolla, Astor, 36

Picasso, Pablo, 108
Pincus, Harry, 16
Pistorius, Steve, 19
Poitier, Sidney, 95
Polisi, Joseph, 46, 74
Powell, Benny, 18
Powell, Bud, 19
Pozo, Chano, 36
Presto, Jenna, 135
Prieto, Dafnis, 171
Printup, Marcus, 67, 74, 75, *107*, *110*, 118, 171, 179, 192
Puente, Tito, 36, 37, 150, 171

R

Rampton, Kenny, *110*, 119
Random House, 184
Rathe, Stephen, 46–47, 89
Rattle, Simon, 59, 185
Rauscher, Frances, 79
Ravel, Maurice, 45
Redd, Vi, 18
Reed, Eric, *28*, 29, 171
Reeves, Dianne, 142, *143*, *147*, 151, 171
Reeves, Karen, 134, 135
Rhythm Road program, 184
Rich, Frank, 175
Ridley, Larry, 18
Riggio, Len, 39
Riley, Ben, 18
Riley, Herlin, 19, *58*, 59, *104*, 105, *125*, 141, 143, *147*, 159, 171, *175*, *195*
Riley, Teddy, 19
Rivers, Sam, 171
Roach, Max, 16, 18, 161, 184

Roberts, Fletcher, 179
Roberts, Marcus, 16, 18, 19, 45, 47, 67, *104*, 105, *111*, 114, 151, 164, *165*, 171, 189
Robinson, David, 90, *114*, *115*, 117, 135, 136
Rockefeller, Nelson, 175
Rodney, Red, 16, 18, 47
Rodriguez, Johnny, 171
Rojas, Nico, 151
Rollins, Sonny, 184
Roney, Wallace, 19, 171
Rose, Charlie, 183
Rose, Frederick P., 83
Rose, Jonathan, 22, 53, 83, *85*, 94
Rosnes, Renee, *28*, 29, 40
Ross, Diana, 157, *160*, 171
Rouse, Charlie, 18
Rubin, Vanessa, 151
Rudin, Jack, 53, 64, 68, 161, 185
Rudin, Susan, 64, 68, 161, 185
Russian National Orchestra, 176
Rutledge, Rosemary, 152

S

Safer, Morley, 179
Sain, Kate, 110
St. Regis hotels, 185
Salonen, Esa-Pekka, 120, *121*
Sanborn, David, 194
Sanon, Jennifer, 171, *188*
Santos, Moacir, 151
Sariahmed, Maya, 134
Schaap, Phil, 78, 134
Schiff, Ashley, *147*, 158, *159*, 161
Schiff, David, 92

Schiff, Lisa, 53, 92, 93, 96, 97, 105, *128*, 131, 144, 183, 185
Schilk, Scott, 135
Schneider, Maria, 171
Scholastic Inc., 67
Scholl, Greg, 197
Schomburg Center, 55
Schroeder, Michele, 67
Schuller, Gunther, 169
Schwartz, Richard, 22
Scofield, John, 171
Scott, Stephen, 171
Sehgal, Kabir, *70*, 71
Sellin, Hervé, 171
September 11th attacks, 93, 118–19, 159
Sgroi, Jay, 135
Shakur, Hassan, *58*, 59
Sheller, Martin, 171
Sherrill, Joya, 171
Shifrin, David, 45, 53
Short, Bobby, 171
Shorter, Wayne, 171
Sickler, Don, 18
Siegel, Janis, 18
Simon, Paul, 145, *148*, 156, 157, 159, 171
Sims, Pete La Roca, 171
60 Minutes, 179, 185
Skaggs, Ricky, 99
Slatkin, Leonard, 184
Smith, Carrie, 18, 159, 171
Smith, Harry, 179
Smith, Jabbo, 169
Smith, Jumaane, 75
Smithsonian Institution, 179, 183
Sneed, Damien, 151

Soloff, Lew, 18, 19
Somerville, Bobby, 135
Spacey, Kevin, 159, 171
Sphere, 16, 18
Stafford, Gregg, 19
Stanley H. Kaplan Penthouse, 15, *45*, 151
Starmer, John, 134
Starwood, 185
Stein, Andy, 18
Stern, David, 158
Stewart, Bob, 19
Stewart, Frank, 190
Stewart, Mark, *156*
Stewart, Sandy, 40, 99
Stoll, Todd, 76, 190
Storyk, John, 89
Stravinsky, Igor, 45, 53
Stripling, Byron, 19
Subway Jazz Orchestra, 55
Suggs, Darian, 135
The Supper Club, *140*, 141
Swing University program, 78

T

Tanaka, Katsuhiko, 171
Tatum, Art, 105
Taylor, Arthur, 19
Taylor, Billy, 161
Taylor, Cecil, 151
Taylor, David, 134
Taylor, James, 145, *146*, 159, 171
Tedeschi, Susan, 159, 171
Temperley, Joe, 18, 19, 71, 105, *110*, 114, 123, *126–27*, *191*, *194*, 195
Terry, Clark, 75

Teter, Christa, *166*, 167
Thompson, Lucky, 192
Time Warner Center, *84*, *85*, *92–93*, 97
Tizol, Juan, 36
Todo Tango, *152*, 153
Townsend, Bross, 18
Tristano, Lennie, 168
Trucks, Derek, 159, *161*, 171
Trueba, Fernando, 36
Turkovic, Milan, 53
Turner, Roslyn, 134
Turney, Norris, 18, 19, 29, 105, 117, 176
Tyner, McCoy, 195

U

Uhl, John, 135
Urbina, Josué, 135

V

Vaché, Warren, 171
Valdés, Bebo, 36, *153*, 171
Valdés, Chucho, 36, 151
Vanity Fair, 179
Vappie, Don, *147*, 175
Vazquez, Papo, 171
Veal, Reginald, 19, *32*, *104*, 105, 159
Viklicky, Emil, 171
Village Vanguard, 161
Viñoly, Rafael, 85, *88*, 89
Vogue magazine, 15, 20, 175
Von Kleist, Erica, 171, *194*, 195

W

Walker, Darren, 159
Walter, Casey, 134
Walton, Cedar, *188*
Wamble, Doug, 171
Ward, Diane, 72, 97, 141
Ward, Geoffrey C., 11, 72, 96, 97, 141
Washington, Kenny, 18, 19
Washington, Peter, 151
Wasserman, Jennie, 135, 136
Watson, Bobby, 151, *178*
WBGO, 16, 176
WeBop, 63, 78, 79, 183, 184
Webster, Ben, 151
Wein, George, 47, 161
Weiss, Michael, 19
Weissberg, Eric, 19
Weissman, George, 15, 20, 22, 30, 161, 181
Weisz, Deborah, 171
Wess, Frank, 18, 19, 46, 47, 189
Westley, Ronald, 28, 29, *170*
Weston, Randy, 47, 99, 171
Westray, Ron, 171
Whitaker, Rodney, *111*, *112*, 151, 171
White, Michael, 16, 19, 175
Whitman, Walt, 20
Wilbur, Bob, *169*
Wilder, Joe, *116*, 117
Williams, Buster, 18
Williams, Claude "Fiddler," 151
Williams, Joe, 168
Williams, Mary Lou, 151
Williams, Robin, *146*
Williams, Todd, 19, *104*, 105, 141, 151

Williams, Vanessa, 159, 171
Willis, Larry, 19
Wilson, August, 157, 171
Wilson, Cassandra, 98, 117, *147*, 171, *180*, 181, 182
Wilson, Joe Lee, 18
Wolfe, Ben, 192, *193*
Wonder, Stevie, 157, 159, 171
Wong, Ho-Mui, 134
Wong, Kaitlyn Falk, 134
Woode, Jimmy, 19, 176
Woodley, Daphnée Saget, 134
Woodman, Britt, 19, 29, 105
Woody Allen Band, *160*
Wright, Eric, 119, 134, 135
Wulkowicz, Molly, 79

Y

Yamin, Eli, 171
Yanofsky, Jon, 134
Young, John, 19

Z

Zorn, John, 151
Zydeco, Buckwheat, *148*